REFLECTIONS ON *MAHARISHI AYURVEDA* AND MENTAL HEALTH

REFLECTIONS ON *MAHARISHI AYURVEDA®* AND MENTAL HEALTH

Four Essays

Jim Brooks, MD

Maharishi University of Management Press

© Jim Brooks 2016 All rights reserved.

Published by
Maharishi University of Management Press
Fairfield, Iowa, United States of America

No part of this publication may be reproduced, stored in a retrieval system, or transmitted, in any form or by any means, electronic, mechanical, photocopying, recording, or otherwise, without the prior permission of the author.

Library of Congress Cataloging-in-Publication Data

ISBN 978-0-923569-71-6

Transcendental Meditation®, TM®, TM-Sidhi®, Maharishi AyurVeda®, Maharishi University of Management, Transcendental Meditation Sidhi, Maharishi Vedic Science, and Consciousness-Based are protected trademarks and are used in the US with permission.

Contents

Foreword by Dr. Robert Schneider ix
Preface xv
Acknowledgments xix
Advisory Note xx

— ESSAY 1 —
Only a New Seed Will Yield a New Crop: A New Paradigm for Mental Health 1

Limitations of the Current Paradigm 5
   1. Biochemical (Biological) Treatments 6
   2. Psychotherapy 8
   3. Behavior Therapies 9
The Human Psyche: A Model from Quantum Physics ... 14
Three Main Goals of Maharishi AyurVeda 22
   1. Prevention of Emotional Imbalance and Mental Illness ... 23
   2. Effective Treatment of Mental Illness 27
   3. Development of Higher States of Human Potential 29

— ESSAY 2 —
Ayurveda and Psychotherapy 37

What Is Therapy? 40
The Patient's Capacity for Insight 44
Maharishi AyurVeda and Therapy 47

Ideal Therapist Qualities 48
   1. Encouragement 56
   2. Patience 59
   3. Knowledge 59
Psychotherapeutic Use of Vedic Literature 69
   1. Encouragement 72
   2. Patience 73
   3. Knowledge 73

— ESSAY 3 —
Sattwa Vijaya: A Balanced Mind Is Victorious   79

Origins of Mental and Emotional Imbalance 83
Ayurvedic (*Sattwa Vijaya*) Treatment Modalities
   for Mental Health 89
Psychological Approach of *Sattwa Vijaya* 90
   1. The Role of Knowledge (*Gyan*) 91
   2. Importance of Memory (*Smriti*) 92
   3. Supportive Component (*Dhairya*) 94
   4. Self-referral Consciousness (*Samadhi*) 95
Physiological Approach of *Sattwa Vijaya* 101
   1. Purification (*Panchakarma*) 102
   2. Herbal and Mineral Compounds (*Dravyaguna*) 102
   3. Dietary Measures (*Aharatattva*) 103
   4. Daily and Seasonal Routines (*Dinacharya*) 104
   5. Exercises for Neuromuscular Integration (*Vyayama*) 106
   6. Neurorespiratory Integration (*Pranayama*) 107
   7. Five Senses Therapy 107
Behavioral Approach of *Sattwa Vijaya* 108

Treatments that Work on the Level of
    Mind, Body, and Spirit 112
Human Physiology: Expression of Veda and
    Vedic Literature 116

— ESSAY 4 —
The Bhagavad-Gita: A Model for Vedic Counseling 119

A Universal Dilemma 122
An Enlightened Guide 125
Knowledge of the Solution 130
Transcending to Relieve Suffering 134
Applying Vedic Principles to Counseling 142
Knowledge (*Gyan* and *Vigyan*) 145
   1. Knowledge of Higher States of Consciousness 147
   2. Knowledge of the Process of Purification 148
   3. Codes of Conduct 149
   4. Knowledge of Personality Types 150
Maharishi AyurVeda Therapies 152
   1. Music Therapy 153
   2. Yoga and Breathing Exercises 154
   3. Knowledge of One's Psycho-physiological Style
      (*Prakriti*) 154
   4. Herbal Therapies 154
Guiding Principles 155

Conclusion 159
About the Author 163

Foreword

Chronic diseases are the leading causes of death and disability in modern society. What are these chronic diseases? Chronic physical disorders include cardiovascular disease, hypertension, and diabetes. At the same time, chronic mental disorders, including depression and anxiety, are leading causes of morbidity, disability, and loss of quality of life. In the United States, the prevalence of mental disorders (including substance abuse) is 30%, affecting nearly one of every three people. However, only one-third of affected individuals are receiving treatment. Far fewer are receiving effective treatment. Interestingly, and relevant to this volume, physical health and mental health are interrelated. For example, cardiovascular disease and mental disorders share at least one common cause — psychological stress. Mental health plays a central role in individual and public health in today's society.

Another major trend in contemporary healthcare is the increasing recognition of iatrogenic disease. A study published by Barbara Starfield at Johns Hopkins University found that 225,000 deaths per year in the United States may be attributed to adverse effects of modern medical care. This ranks modern medicine itself as the third leading cause of death in the United States.

At this time in history, we see the intersections of several trends in health and healthcare:

1. high rates of chronic disorders — both mental and physical, fatal and nonfatal
2. recognition of mental-health factors as a cause or complication of many of these chronic disorders
3. high rates of hazardous side effects of modern healthcare
4. inability of modern medicine to prevent and treat these chronic disorders
5. high cost of medicine threatening individual, family, and societal resources in nearly every country

In response to these limitations of modern healthcare, there has been an explosion of interest in and utilization of complementary and alternative medicine (CAM) in the past several decades. Surveys indicate that approximately 40% of the general public and physicians utilize CAM practices in an effort to treat and prevent chronic mental and physical disorders and to avert adverse effects of conventional medical care.

CAM practices are generally derived from natural medicine systems and principles. The world's oldest traditional system of natural medicine is Ayurveda. Ayurveda has been recognized by the World Health Organization and is considered by many to be the most comprehensive system of natural medicine. It is derived from the ancient Vedic civilization of India. A modern revival of Ayurveda has been conducted by world-renowned Vedic scholar and teacher Maharishi Mahesh Yogi in collaboration with leading Ayurvedic experts, scientists, and physicians and is termed Maharishi AyurVeda®. As eloquently described by Dr. Brooks in this volume, a distinguishing feature of Maharishi AyurVeda is the identification of the field of pure consciousness at the basis of mind and body, and of mental and physical health. Further, this field of pure consciousness is proposed to be identical with the unified field as discovered by unified field theories in quantum physics. Dr. Brooks points out that the classic Ayurveda texts call this level of man and the universe *Atma* or the Self. It is from here that mental health begins.

A second distinguishing feature of Maharishi AyurVeda is the consideration of four domains of health that are interdependent: mind, body, environment, and pure consciousness or the unified field. This range of the domains of influence for health, their interrelationships, theoretical understandings, and applied technologies is elaborated in the 40 branches of Veda and Vedic literature illuminated in their health context by Maharishi AyurVeda. In short, Maharishi AyurVeda is Consciousness-Based℠, holistic medicine in accord with classic Vedic texts. Furthermore, extensive modern scientific research has validated many of the approaches of Maharishi AyurVeda for mental health (and physical health), e.g. anxiety disorders, depression, and stress-related disorders.

The future of medicine lies in integrating the most effective and least harmful methods of healthcare from modern and ancient medical sciences. We anticipate that the Maharishi AyurVeda approach to mental health, or Vedic psychiatry* in the context of medicine, will have a major impact on how medicine understands, prevents, and treats mental disorders. In our new Maharishi Colleges of Perfect Health, medical students will study and practice Vedic psychiatry together with modern medical approaches. This collection of essays will be a resource for this next generation of medical students and physicians.

Vedic psychiatry is an emerging field of integrative medicine. In this collection of essays, Dr. Brooks builds on his extensive clinical experience, consultation with Ayur-

---

* Vedic psychiatry is the branch of Maharishi AyurVeda or Vedic medicine devoted to prevention, treatment, and promotion of mental health. It is a field of healthcare that benefits from time-tested and scientifically validated programs as well as procedures, such as Vedic counseling, that are being developed.

vedic experts, research into the ancient Vedic texts, and his and others' scientific research to illuminate for physicians, psychologists, mental-health practitioners, medical graduate students, professional students, and the general public key elements of this most ancient and most modern approach to mental health.

Kudos to Dr. Brooks for making this set of pioneering contributions to a most important field of health for all.

Robert H. Schneider, MD, FACC
Director, Institute for Natural Medicine and Prevention
Dean, Maharishi College of Perfect Health
Maharishi University of Management
Fairfield, Iowa, USA

References

Clarke T, Black L, Stussman B, Barnes P, Nahin R (2015) National Health Statistics Reports: Trends in the Use of Complementary Health Approaches Among Adults: United States, 2002–2012. In: Centers for Disease Control and Prevention, National Center for Health Statistics, editors: US Dept. of Health and Human Services, pp. 1–9

Hagelin J (1989) Restructuring Physics from its Foundation in Light of Maharishi's Vedic Science. Modern Science and Vedic Science 3: 3–72

Harvard Medical School, Department of Healthcare Policy (2007) National Comorbidity Survey, NSC-R Twelve-Month Prevalence Estimates

Nader T (1995) Human Physiology: Expression of Veda and the Vedic Literature. The Netherlands: Maharishi Vedic University

Schneider R, Charles B, Sands D, Gerace D, Averbach R, Rothenberg S (1997) The Maharishi Vedic Approach to Health and Colleges of Maharishi Vedic Medicine — Creating perfect health for the individual and a disease-free society. Modern Science and Vedic Science 7: 299–315

Schneider R, Fields J (2006) Total Heart Health. Laguna Beach, Calif: Basic Health Publications

Starfield B (2000) Is US Health Really the Best in the World? Journal of the American Medical Association 284: 483–485

Preface

This book is written for those interested in learning how the knowledge of mental health from the East can be integrated with our current knowledge of mental health in the West. I have spent the past 32 years integrating the wisdom of Ayurveda from India with what I have learned in my training as a physician specializing in psychiatry and psychotherapy in the United States. I feel particularly blessed to have studied extensively since 1974 with Maharishi Mahesh Yogi, who during the course of his lifetime restored the knowledge of Ayurveda to its original stature, giving rise to the term 'Maharishi AyurVeda.' In particular, Maharishi reintroduced the importance of having not only the theoretical understanding but also the direct personal experience of pure consciousness as a means to develop higher states of consciousness and ideal health.

The word *Ayurveda* is made up of the Sanskrit *Ayur*, meaning life, and *Veda*, knowledge. The title Maharishi has the word-meaning of great (*Maha*) knower or seer (*Rishi*). Maharishi AyurVeda is thus knowledge of life revitalized for the modern world by a great seer.

Preface

Maharishi defines pure consciousness as the deepest part of ourselves, the essence of who we are. It is the silent field that is the source of our mind, personality, body, and environment. By contacting this field of all possibilities deep within, every aspect of our life is automatically re-enlivened and revitalized, and the result is improved health on every level. The Transcendental Meditation® technique is the method that Maharishi founded and introduced to the world in order for anyone to be able to contact this field of pure consciousness on a regular basis. The technique is easy and effortless, and anyone can learn it and incorporate it into their daily routine. It does not conflict with any religious belief, because it is simply a mechanical mental practice without religious affiliation. I liken it to brushing one's teeth: Brushing regularly, twice a day, keeps the teeth and gums healthy, and prevents the build-up of plaque. Practicing the Transcendental Meditation technique regularly, twice a day, keeps the mind and body healthy, and prevents the build-up of fatigue, stress, and disease. By now, there have been over 600 published studies verifying the health benefits of this most useful and practical technique.

In addition to the Transcendental Meditation technique, Maharishi reintroduced techniques and practices that address the health of a person at every conceivable level. For example, for ideal mental health, Maharishi

Preface

AyurVeda recommends a whole array of therapies. These include music therapy, body-purification therapies, aroma therapy, a daily routine regimen, advanced techniques to develop specific latent mental capacities, herbal and dietary advice, and breathing and exercise routines, to name but a few.

For over 30 years, I have not only been practicing many of these treatment modalities of Maharishi AyurVeda myself, but have been recommending them to my patients. I have found this system of healthcare to be of great benefit both for my own personal growth and well-being, and for the development of health and wholeness for the patients in my medical practice. I see Maharishi AyurVeda as a wonderful complement to my allopathic medical practice, and vice versa.

As I'll discuss in depth in these four essays, my observation is that the current system of mental health, although it is helpful to patients in many ways, is also lacking in some important areas. This is because most current theories and practices primarily address the mental, emotional, and physiological (biochemical) aspects of the person. What Maharishi AyurVeda has to offer is the knowledge and practical techniques for a person to experience him or her self at the very foundation of who they are. Maharishi AyurVeda teaches that underneath all the mental and physiological activity that comprises who we are, there is a silent unified field of pure consciousness. By regularly contacting this field through daily meditation practice, the very foundation of health can be strengthened and enlivened. In addition, the application of many other therapies of Maharishi AyurVeda serves to promote balance and health on all levels of individual and collective life: mental, emotional, physiological, environmental, and spiritual.

This book is a compilation of four separate essays, each one written originally to stand on its own. Each essay takes a slightly different angle on the Vedic approach to mental health. As a result, you may notice certain topics mentioned in more than one essay.

Finally, I sincerely hope that this small book serves to spark your interest in the application of Maharishi AyurVeda to the field of mental health. My hope is that you will choose to add the recommendations of Maharishi AyurVeda to your own health regimen and, if you are a mental-health professional, to your mental-health practice.

Jim Brooks, MD
Fairfield, Iowa, USA
March 25, 2016

Acknowledgments

I would like to acknowledge Maharishi Mahesh Yogi for restoring the total knowledge of natural law to our generation, and for the generations to follow. I can't even begin to imagine how my life would have turned out without his infinite wisdom, guidance, compassion, and unbounded love at every step of the way.

I want to thank the following individuals for their help and encouragement during the various phases of this project, including suggestions, editing, proofreading, book design/typesetting, and cover artwork: Dr. Robert Schneider, Dr. Craig Pearson, Dr. John Hagelin, Dr. Michael Dillbeck, Dr. Patrick Pomfrey, Dr. Sue Brown, Fran Clark, Rob Johnson, Elinor Wolfe, and Harry Bright.

Lastly, I want to give a special thank-you to my wife, Linda, for her support, wisdom, guidance, and love throughout the development and writing of this book.

Advisory Note

This book is designed to introduce the general population and health practitioners alike to the theory and potential practical application of Maharishi AyurVeda in daily life. Programs discussed in the book are not meant as a substitute for any person's regular medical or psychiatric care. Furthermore, it is strongly advised that readers consult with their medical or psychiatric provider prior to adding any Maharishi AyurVeda therapies to their health-treatment protocol. It is particularly important that anyone taking psychiatric or any other medications prescribed by a health provider consult with the health provider prior to changing the dose of or discontinuing the medication.

It is the author's experience that whereas in some instances individuals with a mental-health diagnosis may, in conjunction with the support of their medical provider, be able to reduce the dose or even wean off their allopathic medications, in many instances the best approach is to use Maharishi AyurVeda or other natural treatments in a complementary or supportive way, along with their prescribed medications.

The ideal is to see a medical or mental-health provider who is trained in, or is at least familiar with, Maharishi AyurVeda. If this is not possible, it is encouraged that patients give their provider a copy of this book, and/or other referenced material, so that they might become familiar with how this knowledge can serve as a complement to an existing mental-health regimen. It is also sometimes helpful to encourage your medical provider to speak with another practitioner who is familiar with or has expertise in Maharishi AyurVeda, so that your provider can become better familiarized with the system of natural medicine that you are interested in adding to your healthcare program.

REFLECTIONS ON
MAHARISHI AYURVEDA
AND MENTAL HEALTH

ESSAY 1

Only a New Seed Will Yield a New Crop: A New Paradigm for Mental Health

ESSAY 1

Only a New Seed Will Yield a New Crop: A New Paradigm for Mental Health

It was my mother and father's dream that I should become a doctor. My father was a physician — a fine and compassionate one — and they wanted me to follow suit. I wanted the same thing, and applied to medical school. While I awaited news of my acceptance, I learned to practice the Transcendental Meditation technique because I was interested in natural healthcare. After two years of medical school I told my parents that I wanted to take a year off to become a teacher of the Transcendental Meditation technique and to study natural medicine.

Even though they wanted to be supportive of me, there was a part of them that expected I would go off to some ashram and never return, or return in white robes and, God forbid, that I might not want to be a doctor anymore.

Nonetheless, they put their trust in me, and supported me to take my yearlong sabbatical from medical school. Ironically (from my parents' point of view) it turned out that the knowledge of natural medicine I was able to acquire during that year made me feel more like a real doctor than I would have felt otherwise. I learned about self-healing, about how to give patients information and practical skills they can use to help themselves, not only physically and mentally, but also emotionally and spiritually.

I also learned that without a holistic approach that addresses all aspects of the person (mind, body, and spirit), modern medicine and psychiatry will always fall short of their goals of truly helping people in a complete way. I feel very fortunate that I have had the opportunity to study Maharishi AyurVeda. I have found that this system of natural medicine meets the criteria for being completely holistic in that it addresses all three aspects of the person. I have treated thousands of patients with mental-health issues over the past 30-plus years using Maharishi AyurVeda. The treatment results for most have been extremely positive. Not only have I witnessed consistent symptom reduction, but also greater degrees of energy, vitality, calmness, and joy.

This is a very exciting time in the evolution of the application of Maharishi AyurVeda to the field of modern medicine and psychiatry. Maharishi University of Management (MUM) in Fairfield, Iowa, is embarking on a collaboration with the American University of Integrative Sciences (AUIS) located on St. Maarten in the Caribbean, to offer a dual medical degree track: an MD in modern medicine concurrent with an MS in Maharishi AyurVeda and Integrative Medicine from MUM. These medical students will participate in a system of learning known as Consciousness-Based education, which gives them the intellectual and experiential basis for maximum personal growth.

Limitations of the Current Paradigm

At the present time, the mental-health profession deals with only three aspects of our selves — mind, body, and behavior. If I may oversimplify, "mind" is handled by the various forms of psychotherapy (there are well over 400 styles of therapy), "body" is treated by the pharmacological approach of psychiatry, and "behavior" is the specific domain of the cognitive-behavioral therapies. No school of thought or practice effectively integrates all three approaches. More importantly, the current paradigm of modern psychiatry misses the most essential aspect of our nature, the Self or pure consciousness, the deepest level of what we are at our source. This paradigm is unaware of the fundamental aspect of our nature, pure consciousness — our essential spiritual nature at the core of our being.

Let's consider the three standard approaches, and then explore the missing dimension.

1. Biochemical (Biological) Treatments

The use of psychoactive drugs is one of the three primary modes of treatment in the mental-health field today. For some people, these drugs have been a virtual miracle. They have allowed many people with serious problems to live outside a hospital setting. They have provided enough relief of symptoms that people can function more effectively both socially and occupationally. For example, one relatively new drug, clozapine, an anti-schizophrenia medication, now effectively treats one-third of people who, just a few years ago, were considered untreatable. In addition, tens of millions of prescriptions are written every year for drugs that help relieve insomnia or calm jangled nerves.

Unfortunately, these medications frequently bring side effects. Headaches, nausea, dry mouth, constipation, blurred vision, and symptoms that resemble Parkinson's disease often accompany psychiatric medications. One particularly unfortunate side effect of antipsychotic medications is tardive dyskinesia. This is a potentially irreversible neurological condition that is characterized by involuntary rhythmical movements of the mouth, facial muscles, and extremities.

Some medicines used to treat one mental symptom can cause other mental symptoms; for example, antipsychotic medications useful in treating schizophrenia may result in depression. It is common to treat the side effects of one medicine with another medicine, but the second may also have side effects of its own that have to be treated, often with yet a third medicine. This is so common that it is virtually standard practice.[1]

In addition to symptomatic side effects, patients often become dependent upon certain medicines, in particular those used for treating panic attacks and other anxiety disorders.

According to Herman van Praag, former chairman of the psychiatry department at Albert Einstein Medical School in New York, "There's been an overestimation of what biological treatments can contribute to the treatment of psychiatric disorders. The idea that you can fix it with a drug is an oversimplification; you have to treat psychological issues, too."[2]

2. Psychotherapy

The second major mode of treatment consists of various "talk" therapies. Here, the client is encouraged to examine with the therapist personal problems and conflicts and to work through past hurts, resentments, and traumas. By expressing how they feel, patients can release some of their internal pressure and reduce the emotional and psychological blocks creating distress in their lives. Also, through discussion with the therapist, they can gain insight into the inner sources of their difficulties, and explore ways to overcome those difficulties. These "talking cures" have also been effective for interpersonal relationships, helping people resolve conflicts and other problems.[3]

Some studies suggest that success in therapy comes in part from the method being used, but also from the personal qualities (insight, communication skills, compassion, empathy, etc.) of both therapist and client. According to Dr. Sol Garfield, a research psychologist at Washington University, "Research shows that the things that used to be considered superficial and insignificant — such as faith in the therapist, the expectation of being helped, encouragement, suggestion — are among the important factors that lead to improvement."[4]

In recent years there has been an explosion of newer psychotherapeutic modalities, both for helping relieve major psychological issues, and for personal growth and development. Even compared to 10 years ago, some of these methodologies achieve profound inner transformation in a relatively short time. Voice Dialogue, Shadow Work, and Emotionally Focused Therapy are a few examples of these newer modalities.

3. Behavior Therapies

The third type of treatment is behavioral therapy. This modality attempts to directly alter an undesirable behavior pattern. Initially behavioral therapy was used primarily in specific conditions, such as when a person suffered from a fear of heights, or other phobias. But it has evolved to deal with more subtle levels of the psyche, and now aims to help people transform not only behavior but also patterns of thinking and emotions.

Cognitive Behavioral Therapy, for example, developed and popularized by Drs. Aaron Beck, David Burns, and Donald Meichenbaum among others, helps people gain insight into their automatic thought patterns and hidden belief systems. It helps them "reprogram" so that they replace self-defeating patterns with more positive thinking and behavior.

This approach can be useful in many situations. It is possible to monitor our thoughts and feelings, and we can, in some circumstances, simply decide not to give in to negative feelings or destructive thought patterns. Instead we can learn to "shift gears" and think more positively and constructively.

One reason for the success of Cognitive Behavioral Therapy is that it directly involves the client or patient in the process of growing out of problems. If the process is to succeed, the individual must learn some basic principles, study himself or herself, and actively apply what he or she has learned. This develops self-sufficiency, which in itself is a step in the direction of growth.

One limitation of Cognitive Behavioral Therapy is that it does not deal with intra-psychic elements — there is little or no attempt at a deeper understanding of the cause of one's self-defeating or negative behaviors. Also, the biological aspect is not always accounted for, so if there is any significant physical imbalance causing or complicating the problem, it may not be fully corrected by cognitive behavior approaches.

All three of these methods of treatment have their own usefulness and value. As we shall see, Maharishi AyurVeda does not invalidate any of them, but rather serves to enhance all three. For example, it offers guidelines to make talk therapy more effective, suggesting ways to inspire and uplift the patient and to improve the skill of the therapist.

In the area of cognitive behavior therapy, Ayurveda offers literally hundreds of "Behavioral Rasayanas." The Sanskrit word *Rasayana* means "rejuvenation." The Behavioral Rasayanas are guidelines to organize our daily activities and routines to create or restore a state of balanced mental health. A few examples of Behavioral Rasayanas are "treat your elders, parents, and teachers respectfully," and "don't speak badly of others." These guidelines can also be consciously applied to increase harmony and communication in relationships. Later in this book is a more extensive discussion about the various health benefits of Behavioral Rasayanas.

Biological treatment in Ayurveda touches a dimension that is only now coming to the attention of Western medicine. Physiological knowledge in the West has been restricted to the level known to classical physics (i.e. the biochemical level). Maharishi AyurVeda, however, appears to operate in the quantum mechanical dimension, the aspect of our physiology that is more subtle and underlies the gross physical structure. Ayurvedic natural approaches, which operate at the quantum level, have a holistic and balancing effect on the body as a whole.

Maharishi AyurVeda goes beyond mind, body, and behavior to their deeper, common source — consciousness, pure intelligence, the Self. From there, as we shall see, all three of these aspects of our lives can be influenced spontaneously, with the full force of nature's intelligence.

A drawback of our current system of mental healthcare is its failure to evolve effective methods of prevention. It does not prevent people from becoming anxious or depressed or developing mental illness in the first place. Nor is there, outside the small percentage of professionals involved in the human potential movement, any attempt to understand what Abraham Maslow called "the further reaches of human nature" — our capacity for increased intelligence, creativity, insight, intuition, love, happiness, and inner peace.

At the present time, the predominant focus of the mental-health profession is the treatment of mental imbalance. Indeed, mental and emotional dysfunction and imbalance are so prevalent that there is really no time to promote health. Professionals have been so busy "putting out fires" that they've had no time or energy to educate the public in fire-safety rules.

Even if some therapists have wanted to focus on this aspect of mental health, the sad fact is that they have lacked the knowledge of how to do so. The knowledge of prevention, including a coherent vision of higher stages of human development and how to encourage their unfoldment, is not well understood. Traditionally this knowledge has not been included in our training as mental-health professionals. As the Swiss psychiatrist Carl G. Jung pointed out, we in the Western world have learned to "tame and subject the psyche, but we know nothing about its methodical development ... For this we must have knowledge of a way or a method — and so far we have known of none."[5]

Therefore, advances are very much needed. This should not be surprising, since the field is still in its infancy. As a medical discipline, psychiatry is barely 100 years old. Sigmund Freud, the pioneer of Western psychiatry and psychotherapy, published his first independent work in 1900. Half a century later, Jung lamented that

> we have to acknowledge that we have as yet no fully satisfactory conception of the nature of the neurosis nor of the principles of treatment ... we are still far from having anything like a thorough knowledge of the human psyche.[6]

I don't believe that mental-health professionals today would seriously object to Jung's opinion. Fortunately, Maharishi AyurVeda offers a new perspective on the human psyche that can potentially revolutionize the field of mental health.

The Human Psyche: A Model from Quantum Physics

One limitation in the training of mental-health professionals today is that they are rarely taught to see the full possibility and range of human development. This can result in an incomplete view of the client and a limited understanding of the person's capacity for mental health.

Freud began modern psychiatry and psychotherapy by looking below the surface of life into the hidden realms of the psyche. His discoveries and insights, and the contributions of his followers, were profound and helpful, but there is a great need to look more deeply.

It is as if Freud, and many great psychologists and psychiatrists after him, surveyed a building. They even looked into the basement, but they missed the foundation. The building is obvious and above the ground, and the basement may contain some interesting relics of the past, but the foundation is hidden from view. Yet it is fundamental — the entire building is based upon it. All the floors are tied to it and refer to it for their strength and stability. For the building to be strong, the foundation must be strong.

The mental-health field today deals with only the mind, body, and behavior. Maharishi AyurVeda offers knowledge of an added dimension — the Self, the underlying pure consciousness of the individual. This is the most fundamental dimension that underlies the personality, mostly overlooked by Western psychology.

As Maharishi explains, the Self, pure consciousness, is the foundation upon which the entire edifice of our conscious life is constructed. If we are not able to refer to that invisible inner source of strength and fullness, problems will inevitably arise, as cracks will appear in the walls when a building's foundation is weak.

Just as the physical sciences previously limited their sphere of investigation to the measurable, material realms of physical creation, Western psychology has dealt only with mind, body and behavior. Now, however, with the advent of quantum theory, hailed by many physicists as the most useful and accurate theory in science, knowledge of a greater range of life is becoming available. Physicists, mathematicians, and other scientists are learning about the intangibles and invisibles. The mental-health profession must keep pace with the other sciences, if it is to base its treatment on the most holistic understanding of the human psyche.

Over the past two decades, researchers have made giant strides towards verifying the hypothesis of Albert Einstein and many other great scientists: that the entire universe emerges from one fundamental field. All the force fields (such as gravity and electromagnetism) and all the matter fields (the sub-atomic particles), which together form the basis of all things and their interactions, now appear to be the expression or manifestation of one underlying, unmanifest, unified field.

According to unified field theories, the entire diversified universe is built of something even more fundamental and refined than atoms and energy fields. That "something" is completely beyond the range of measurability — it is smaller than the smallest possible observation, and cannot be perceived by the senses or the technological extensions of the senses. It is completely out of the physical universe, transcendental and unmanifest. And yet, according to the mathematical calculations of some of the greatest scientific minds of our time, it is there.

What these "unified field theories" suggest is that the entire universe, from electrons and quarks to the movements of stars and galaxies, has its basis not in particles or even energies, but in a completely invisible, non-material, non-changing, silent field. And because everything in the universe obeys natural laws — from gravity to the laws of biological growth and chemical interaction — that field must be the source not only of things, but also of the laws that govern things, the laws of nature. The unified field therefore must be a field of power and intelligence so enormous that it can create and organize everything on all levels of the universe at every moment. This is analogous to how our DNA is the underlying basis of our entire physiology. It is the silent basis of all the activity that manifests as a result of its very existence.

In recent years some scientists, including Paul Davies, Heinz Pagels, and C.H. Llewellyn Smith, have suggested that such "subjective" qualities as intelligence, dynamism, and attributes of self-awareness and self-interaction, appear to exist at the quantum level. Dr. John Hagelin, one of the world's leading quantum physicists, suggests that the unified field is a field of pure subjectivity that is the foundation of the entire manifested objective world. According to Hagelin, "The defining characteristics of the unified field are identical to the essential characteristics of pure consciousness."[7] Remarkably, this description of the nature of life directly parallels the ancient Vedic view.

Maharishi AyurVeda embraces the discoveries of modern science and integrates them with the teachings of the Vedic seers who originally developed Ayurveda. In Maharishi AyurVeda, the unified field (sometimes referred to as *Atma*, the Self, or *Brahm*, Totality) is directly equated with the Self. Just as there is silence at the basis of all dynamism in the universe (the unified field is a field of non-activity) so there is silence at the basis of all mental activity. By allowing the conscious mind to settle down to its least excited state, we are able to experience that silence.

That non-active but alert inner wakefulness is the Self. It is the innermost being of each and every one of us. We are not merely time- and space-bound personalities. In our deepest essence, deeper than the various aspects of our personalities, we are unbounded, infinitely creative, and at one with the organizing power of the universe.

Between the silence of the Self and the solid structure of the physical body lies the quantum dimension. Physics describes quantum mechanics as the world of quarks and mesons, of energy fields and fine particles. It is where the unified field begins to manifest as the finest impulses of energy and matter, which then unfold into material objects. Dr. Hagelin has postulated that the quantum level of existence includes not only quantum waves, particles, and energy fields, but also the realm of mental functioning.[8] The quantum physicist Roger Penrose has also hypothesized mathematical models that may correlate the quantum field to mind and consciousness.[9] Author Peter Baksa gives a nice summary of the quantum mechanical nature of the mind in an article entitled "Can Our Brainwaves Affect Our Physical Reality?"[10]

Hagelin's model precisely defines three distinct but

interrelated levels of human life. The first is the unified field or "superstring," sometimes referred to as Self, Soul, Spirit, or *Atma*. It is the foundation for the manifestation of the other two. The next level is the quantum mechanical level, which includes not only fine particles and energy fields, but also the whole realm of mental functioning. This means that thoughts are very refined quanta of energy that are directional and have a discrete wave function. The most manifest level of ourselves is the actual physical level, our brain and body and all its measurable components. So Maharishi AyurVeda, in essence, is a system of healthcare that operates holistically on the level of mind, body, and spirit.

By enlivening the source, the unified field, we can influence the entire system in one stroke. This is the secret of the effectiveness of Maharishi AyurVeda: it operates from the level of intelligence that governs the whole.

In Maharishi AyurVeda, healing takes place on the unified field level with the Transcendental Meditation and Transcendental Meditation Sidhi[SM] programs (the TM-Sidhi® program is an advanced program of Transcendental Meditation). Healing also takes place on the quantum level. The quantum level of healing refers to treatment modalities that address the subtle vibratory impulses of the mind and body. Some examples of treatments that address this quantum level include Gandharva Veda, Vedic Sound therapies, Jyotish (medical astrology) and Yagya (Vedic recitation), herbal treatments, etc. Of course, when the focus is on balancing the deepest, most powerful levels of the person, then it follows that profound transformation will naturally occur on the more expressed, more manifest level of the physical body as well. This is validated by hundreds of published studies on the health benefits of Maharishi AyurVeda.

Modern medicine is beginning to recognize that the mind plays a role in the origin of all sorts of diseases. It is now known, for example, that:

- chronic anger increases the risk of heart disease,
- depression decreases immunity,
- optimists live longer than pessimists,
- women with breast cancer who participate in group psychotherapy generally live longer than women who do not, and
- learning to relax can improve fertility.

A decade or two ago, such statements would have made most physicians scoff. Today, however, a whole field of medicine, psychoneuroimmunology, is developing to study such phenomena. It is now known, for example, that the immune system and central nervous system are intimately connected. This view is completely contrary to the traditional medical model that has seen them as two separate and independent systems.

According to Robert Ader of the University of Rochester School of Medicine, "It's an historical accident that we talk about an immune system, a nervous system, and an endocrine system. It reflects our ignorance. Before, we divided up our studies into these different systems. But they aren't different. The fact is, the organism responds as a whole."[11]

Ayurveda has described this holistic nature of the human physiology for at least 5000 years. It teaches that the entire system can be maintained in good health from a central pivot point deeper than the mind — the innermost Self.

All the modalities of Maharishi AyurVeda aim at enlivening pure consciousness, the underlying basis of the whole mind–body system. This is the essence of healing: nourishing the whole person from that deepest level. This is the fulfillment of mind–body medicine, the ultimate application of the principle of "mind over matter."

Because psychological theory has until now failed to grasp the full depth and dignity of the human being, our treatment methods have been partial and incomplete, never effecting needed enlivenment at a fundamental level.

With the expanded understanding of life provided by Maharishi AyurVeda, we can now truly begin to treat the whole person.

Three Main Goals of Maharishi AyurVeda

As Thoreau said, "In the long run, men hit only what they aim at. Therefore … they had better aim at something high."[12] One of the reasons the mental-health profession has had only limited success is that its goals are too limited. As I have pointed out, the primary preoccupation of the field until now has been the understanding and treatment of disease. This is only one of three main goals of Maharishi AyurVeda for the field of mental and emotional health. The three goals are:

1. prevention of emotional imbalance and mental illness,
2. effective treatment of mental and emotional problems when the need arises, and
3. development of higher states of human potential.

Now let's consider each of these goals, and the approaches used in Maharishi AyurVeda to fulfill them.

1. Prevention of Emotional Imbalance and Mental Illness

As mentioned above, Ayurveda strongly emphasizes prevention. There is an ancient Sanskrit saying that is an Ayurvedic motto: "Avert the danger that has not yet come." The aim is to make preventive measures available on a broad scale, both for professionals to use in their practices, and for individuals to utilize on their own.

Numerous common psychological disturbances — insomnia, anxiety, worry, depression, stress, fears and inhibitions, and self-destructive habits — all detract from the quality of life. They reduce effectiveness, interfere with relationships, and greatly diminish the joy of living. More severe mental imbalance is painful and life-disturbing, both to the person experiencing it and to those around him or her. Surely all efforts should be made to prevent the occurrence of these problems. Yet in the field of mental health, prevention has been a relatively unexplored and undeveloped field. By contrast, Maharishi AyurVeda takes as its first goal the prevention of stress, anxiety, physiological imbalance, and all the feelings and behaviors that lead to psychological problems.

Most people believe that they have no control over their mental health. As a culture, we seem to feel that emotional turbulence, instability, and mental illness just come upon us, like a cold or the flu, and that there's not much we can do about it. This commonly held belief breeds a kind of helplessness.

Actually, there is a lot we can do. Prevention is a fast-growing, increasingly accepted field of medicine that emphasizes personal responsibility and personal choice in the process of maintaining good health. The American Cancer Society and the American Heart Association, among others, now urge us to get proper exercise and sufficient rest, eat a balanced and healthy diet, quit smoking, and so on. Following these guidelines for healthy living keeps the physiology strong and makes us less susceptible to disease.

It is commonly observed that out of a group of people who may be exposed to the same germs, only a few will actually become sick. Similarly, even when people have a genetic predisposition to a particular illness, it is not necessary or inevitable that they develop it. For example, the children of a schizophrenic parent have an increased risk of developing schizophrenia, but not all the children in a particular family will do so. This is true even of twins — despite an identical gene structure, often if one of the twins develops schizophrenia, the other will not.

This variability occurs because there are always a number of components involved in throwing the system out of balance. Some of these, such as genetic factors, we cannot control. But often, we do have control over quite a number of others, such as our diet, living environment, our attitude, and how we manage stress. Whether or not we exercise that control is up to us.

Because prevention has until now been an under-emphasized, under-funded, and indeed virtually unexplored area in the mental-health field, people have simply not realized that they could exercise control over their state of emotional and mental health. In my opinion it is time for this misunderstanding to become ancient history.

Many methodologies of Maharishi AyurVeda have already been proven effective as preventive medicine. A study in the journal *Psychosomatic Medicine,* utilizing statistics of the Blue Cross/Blue Shield insurance companies, showed that people practicing the Transcendental Meditation technique (a key stress-management method of Maharishi AyurVeda) had a 50% reduction in both inpatient and outpatient medical-care utilization. They had 87% less hospitalization for heart disease and nervous-system disorders, and 73% less for nose, throat, and lung disorders and psychological disorders. More dramatically, people over 40, who generally suffer from ill health more often, had 69% fewer inpatient days and 74% fewer outpatient visits.[13]

Reflections on *Maharishi AyurVeda* and Mental Health

The Swedish government's National Health Board conducted a nationwide study more than 30 years ago. They found that hospital admissions for psychiatric care were 150 to 200 times less common among the 35,000 practitioners of the Transcendental Meditation technique in Sweden than for the population as a whole.[14]

Maharishi AyurVeda offers dozens of preventive measures, from diet and exercise recommendations to daily routines, guidelines for harmonious relationships, and stress management procedures. For example, when the weather is hot, eating spicy foods, taking hot baths, and sitting in the sun would tend to generate an imbalance. This could lead to an "overheated" mental/emotional state characterized by impatience, anger, and so on. With just a little knowledge, and the willingness to apply it, it is possible and easy to "cool" the system and restore a balanced state of mind and body. When the system is in balance, instability and illness are much less likely to take root.

In the 1990s, the slogan of the National Institutes of Health was "Health for all by 2000." Sadly, that goal was never achieved, because until now the focus has been on treating disease instead of preventing it. This type of societal change is possible, but it can only be achieved through the development and widespread adoption of methods of prevention.

2. Effective Treatment of Mental Illness

Many physicians, such as Bernie Siegel, Larry Dossey, and Joan Borysenko, have recently begun to talk about our inner intelligence and the self-healing capacities of the human being. The late Norman Cousins, although not a physician, was one of the early pioneers in bringing what is now being called "mind–body medicine" to the public. His books, *Anatomy of an Illness*, *The Healing Heart*, and others, reviewed the scientific research indicating that we have a powerful capacity to heal ourselves from within.

Cousins, stricken with a life-threatening illness, proved this theory on himself. Based on evidence that happiness strengthens the immune system and promotes health and healing, while unhappiness depresses immune functioning, Cousins centered his self-designed healing program on a kind of laughter therapy. He embarked on viewing old Candid Camera programs, Marx Brothers movies, and other laughter-provoking material. His plan was effective — his full recovery gave him more than a decade of creative and productive life.[15]

Cases of "spontaneous remission" of serious diseases such as cancer are well known but little understood. There are innumerable stories of cures that are inexplicable to science. These self-healings, according to the principles of Maharishi AyurVeda, are not random events. They are based on aligning the individual's inner intelligence with the deep universal intelligence and self-repair functioning inherent in the body.

Maharishi AyurVeda applies this knowledge of the organism's self-healing capacity to the mind, utilizing safe, natural procedures to stimulate the innate intelligence of the system for the prevention and cure of mental illness and the promotion of emotional well-being.

One of the lessons from this natural healing system is that people are capable of taking responsibility for the prevention of illness by using intelligent, commonsense preventive measures such as stress management, proper diet, gaining sufficient rest. This is the way that healing occurs quickly and lastingly. If treatments are imposed from outside, such as shock treatment or medication, and the patient is not actively involved, symptoms may be temporarily alleviated, but no genuine cure is likely to occur.

It has been my experience that there comes a time in most people's struggles with emotional pain or imbalance that they recognize and accept that the real healing is up to them. They realize that if they don't make the decision to get better, and act on that decision, there will be no real progress.

Maharishi AyurVeda provides a person who has made that decision with many wonderful options of treatment modalities that can be undertaken on one's own, independent of any doctors, trainers, or therapists. Such practices as meditation, Yoga postures, self-massage, and dietary regulation are quickly and easily learned, enjoyable, and simple to practice on one's own.

Most people are excited to try these non-addictive, safe, yet powerful procedures. In employing them, they feel they are taking responsibility for their own progress, their own self-healing — and indeed they are. This makes the decision to take charge of one's own healing much easier, because it no longer seems like a difficult, impossible, or painful project.

3. Development of Higher States of Human Potential

Psychiatry and the allied mental-health professions should not stop short at preventing and treating disease. Rather, they should include the spiritual development of the individual in the treatment plan.

All the efforts of psychiatry have been directed to the relatively small portion of the population who develop mental illness. What about the others? Are they truly happy and fulfilled in their lives? The answer, of course, is no — fulfillment is not the common experience. Shouldn't the mental-health profession have something to offer this relatively healthy "silent majority" as well?

It is an important Ayurvedic principle that as human beings, we all possess a powerful urge to expand beyond the present boundaries of our circumstances. This is experienced both as greater outward achievement and as more inner development such as acquiring new knowledge, gaining new skills, or practicing techniques like meditation to promote a deeper inner experience.

The ability to continually expand our boundaries brings a sense of freedom and happiness. As a person grows and becomes more capable of progressing smoothly and easily on his or her own path in life, there is room in the heart for patience, love, and generosity toward others. In contrast, the inability to progress makes one feel frustrated, angry, and unhappy. Thus, something as simple as the inspiration and self-esteem that come from personal growth and the fulfillment of one's aspirations can eliminate many of the psychological ills that beset men and women today.

The ability to grow is not so much dependent upon our outer circumstances as upon our inner creative intelligence. What is needed, therefore, is a systematic way to unfold more of each person's latent capabilities, an area in which Maharishi AyurVeda has the most to offer.

"Jerry," a 42-year-old businessman, was someone who would be considered "healthy" and quite "normal" by the standards of the medical and mental-health professions. Yet, like so many people in our society, he wasn't happy. I'm not sure how many seminars, trainings, and so on he tried before I met him. When he learned to practice the Transcendental Meditation technique he said, "I immediately felt better in every way. I began to sleep better, I was happier, I had more energy, and I began to feel easier inside as if a great load had been lifted from my shoulders. Needless to say, these benefits began to affect everything I did — my job, my ability to accomplish things and most of all, my relationships with friends and family."

What "Jerry" gained from his practice of Transcendental Meditation inspired him to try other aspects of Maharishi AyurVeda. Looking back, he spoke of "the growth of wholeness and stability that I have enjoyed over the years through Transcendental Meditation and the other techniques of Maharishi AyurVeda. Each one seemed to mark an increase of freedom from a psychological or physical boundary that restricted my life in some way."

Human development is virtually unlimited. Growth in intelligence, understanding, insight, awareness, and creativity can go on almost indefinitely. Research is now revealing that mental potential can continue to unfold well into adulthood and even old age.

Ideal mental health requires a healthy, balanced

physiology, emotional openness, vulnerability, richness of feeling, and full development of the mind. By full development of the mind I mean the ability to use one's intelligence, creativity, understanding, and intuition to one's full extent and power. Ideal mental health means to truly know one's whole self, not just the outer aspects of mind and personality, not just thoughts, feelings, memories, and desires. It means knowing one's deepest nature as well — the hidden silent center of our being, the unbounded, eternal bliss consciousness of the Self.

Throughout the ages, the goal of spiritual traditions has been the ability to experience this deepest core of our being at all times. To know the truth about our existence, to know the greatness of who we really are, naturally confers self-esteem and self-confidence, inner stability, courage, and release from fear of all kinds. It bestows happiness and fulfillment. This, in essence, is what many traditions refer to as "enlightenment."

An ancient Chinese text[16] describes the enlightened, self-realized person as

> *one who without effort hits upon what is right, and without thinking understands what he wants to know, whose life is easily and naturally in harmony.*

Only a New Seed Will Yield a New Crop

The Bhagavad-Gita, one of the classics of Vedic literature, says that the self-realized person, "whose happiness is within, whose contentment is within, whose light is all within,"[17] is so fulfilled and contented that:

> *there is no action that he need do.*
> *Neither has he any profit to gain ...*
> *from the actions he has done;*
> *or from the actions he has not done: nor*
> *is there any living creature on whom*
> *he need rely for any purpose.*[18]

The American poet Walt Whitman spoke glowingly of the state of enlightenment, stating that in such a person:

> there is not left any vestige of despair or misanthropy or cunning or exclusiveness ... [he] hardly knows pettiness or triviality ... he is complete in himself.[19]

Until mental-health professionals not only address the treatment of mental illness, but also offer knowledge and practical methods to help all men and women grow to be truly fulfilled and satisfied in their lives, the profession will not have matured to its full dignity or stature. Attaining this level of mental health is possible through the application of the principles of Maharishi AyurVeda.

Notes

1. Daniel Goleman, "Critics Challenge Reliance on Drugs in Psychiatry," in *New York Times* (October 17, 1989), B7.
2. Herman van Praag, quoted in ibid.
3. According to Dr. T. Byram Darasu at Albert Einstein Medical College, in "The Talking Cure Today," *World Monitor* (August 1989).
4. Sol E. Garfield and Allen Bergin, "Person Therapy, Outcome and Some Therapist Variables," in *Psychotherapy: Theory, Research and Practice* (Fall 1971), 253.
5. C.G. Jung, *Modern Man in Search of a Soul* (New York, USA: Harcourt, Brace and World, 1962), 53–54.
6. Ibid., 55.
7. John Hagelin, quoted in *Science and Technology of the Unified Field Course Syllabus*, Physics Course, Lesson 1 (Maharishi International University, 1990).
8. John Hagelin, "Is Consciousness the Unified Field?" presentation at Science and Nonduality Conference, 2014 http://www.scienceandnonduality.com/videos/john-hagelin-is-consciousness-the-unified-field/
9. Roger Penrose, *The Large, the Small, and the Human Mind* (UK: Cambridge University Press, 1997).
10. Peter Baksa, "Can Our Brainwaves Affect Our Physical Reality?" in *Huffpost Healthy Living* (November 26, 2011).

11. Robert Ader, Dept. of Psychiatry, University of Rochester School of Medicine, "Psychoneuroimmunology" in *Yearbook of Science and Technology* (New York, 1995).
12. Henry David Thoreau, *Walden* (1854).
13. David Orme-Johnson, "Medical Care Utilization and the Transcendental Meditation Program," *Psychosomatic Medicine* 49 (1987), 493–507.
14. J. Suurkula, "The Transcendental Meditation Technique and the Prevention of Psychiatric Illness," (Vasa Hospital, University of Gothenburg: Sweden, 1977).
15. Rene Dubos, "Introduction," in Norman Cousins, *Anatomy of an Illness as Perceived by the Patient: Reflections on Healing and Regeneration* (New York: Bantam, 1981), 15.
16. Confucius, "The Golden Mean of Tsesze," in *The Wisdom of China and India*, ed. Lin Yutang (New York: Modern Library, 1942), 856.
17. Maharishi Mahesh Yogi, *Maharishi Mahesh Yogi on the Bhagavad-Gita, A New Translation and Commentary, Chapters 1–6* (Penguin Books, 1967/1990), Chapter V, verse 24.
18. Ibid., Chapter III, verses 17–18.
19. Walt Whitman, Preface to 1855 edition of *Leaves of Grass*.

REFLECTIONS ON
MAHARISHI AYURVEDA
AND MENTAL HEALTH

ESSAY 2

Ayurveda and Psychotherapy

ESSAY 2

Ayurveda and Psychotherapy

It's commonly thought that therapy and counseling are rather new practices, perhaps a hundred years old (when Freud first developed psychoanalysis). Actually, the whole concept of psychotherapy is thousands of years old. The Ayurvedic textbooks describe the great importance of the relationship between doctor and patient. The verbal and non-verbal communication that flows back and forth is considered to have enormous healing potential. In the Vedic literature there are numerous accounts of how, just through dialogue alone, an individual can be brought out of the depths of depression or anxiety. Through the study of these healing encounters one can extract knowledge, principles, and methods that have great application in the field of mental health today.

The concept of psychotherapy in Ayurveda goes well

beyond just talk therapy. It involves a wide variety of somatic techniques for enlivening mental and emotional well-being. These include diet, exercise, daily oil massage, body purification, music- and aroma-therapies, herbs, meditation, and a variety of other treatments, all designed to holistically enhance mental health. Many of these are discussed in detail in the other essays in this book. The psychotherapist trained in Maharishi AyurVeda utilizes an integrated approach that includes these *and* the healing value of dialogue. This chapter primarily deals with the psychotherapeutic value that results from application of the principles of Maharishi AyurVeda in a counseling setting.

Whereas in the mental-health field today the focus is primarily on reducing symptoms, Maharishi AyurVeda offers mental-health professionals an opportunity both to help alleviate symptoms and to help a person recognize his or her fullest human potential.

What Is Therapy?

Before going into the Ayurvedic approaches, it might be helpful to explore three questions, namely, "What is therapy or counseling?", "What are the different types?", and "How are they different from each other?"

Usually therapy involves two people, the therapist

and the patient or client, but it can also involve couples, families, or a group of individuals with a common focus (such as a "depression group" or a "women's issues group"). Through the therapy process, or the dynamic interaction between the individuals, there is the hope for a positive outcome, such as greater insight; less anger, depression, or anxiety; less addictive tendencies; improved relationships.

During the past several decades, many types of therapy have been developed. In 1978 Parloff reported[1] that there were 140 different therapy modalities being practiced at that time. Since then the number has grown even larger! Although it's very difficult to find order in such a morass of diversity, Karasu[2] did a remarkable job of looking for underlying themes to categorize therapy modalities. He narrowed the categories to three: dynamic, behavioral, and experiential.

Dynamic therapy aims at helping a person discover the underlying causes of his or her emotional distress. There is an attempt to explore a person's current problems in the light of one's past. It is assumed that current symptoms are in large part due to unresolved, largely unconscious, conflicts from one's childhood. Treatment consists of gaining insight into how one's past is impacting the present. This "making the unconscious conscious" is felt to be the main curative element.

Since Freud there have been numerous contributions to psychoanalytic theory and technique. In this type of counseling the therapist is there primarily as a silent witness, who expresses insight at crucial moments in the therapeutic process. He or she is a catalyst whose purpose is to facilitate self-discovery, catharsis, and self-exploration on the part of the patient.

Behavioral therapy, or the more recently developed Cognitive Behavioral Therapy, is based on learning theory. Basically, a person's thinking and behavior are thought to be the result of learned behavior. If one is afraid of heights, then this is likely due to having learned this at some earlier point in one's life. As an example, perhaps one slipped and fell off a roof at a young age, which led to a subsequent fear of heights. In this type of counseling, in contrast to the dynamic style mentioned above, the past reasons for one's symptoms are felt to be relatively unimportant. What is important is to re-learn thinking or behavior that is more normal and healthy. The counselor is much more active in this type of therapy. He or she is seen as a coach or educator, helping the client in the re-training process. Research on this type of therapy has indicated benefit in treating milder forms of anxiety and depression (the more severe forms usually require a combination of therapy and medication). This is probably the most popular form of therapy today because it is problem-focused and more short-term than dynamically oriented therapy. Hence it is generally more cost effective.

Experiential therapies differ philosophically from the Freudian model in that they tend to be more humanistic. That is, they tend to see human beings as intrinsically healthy, and have less of a defeatist or deterministic viewpoint. Freud and many of his followers thought that we are basically subservient to our unconscious drives and impulses. In experiential therapies, however, there is more of an emphasis on experiencing and drawing out our latent creative potentialities. Many of these approaches recognize that we have not only an individual nature but also a more universal aspect that links us to others and our environment. Jungian therapy is an example. Jung believed that we all have access to a "collective unconscious" consisting of archetypes — universal tendencies inherited from generations past — such as monarch, warrior, mother, father. Shadow Work and Voice Dialogue are experiential, post-modern Jungian-based methods of personal growth and psychotherapy respectively. These methodologies help individuals access their inner archetypal energies to transform old, outdated belief patterns and repressed emotions. This results in a healthier expression and more loving viewpoint of oneself.

Reflections on *Maharishi AyurVeda* and Mental Health

Abraham Maslow was another highly regarded experiential psychologist who believed that happy, well balanced, and successful individuals had "transcending" experiences, during which time they experienced their unbounded, universal nature. These experiences, according to Maslow, helped people tap into a source of inner creative energy, allowing them to function more closely to their full potential.

Karasu divided the experiential therapies into three categories (although some methodologies like Shadow Work are seen to incorporate elements of all three):

1. Philosophical — involving verbal techniques (Jung, Rogers)
2. Somatic — with a focus on experiencing physical and emotional release (Janov's primal scream, gestalt therapy, etc.)
3. Spiritual — involving methods that seek to give direct experience of one's transcendental or spiritual nature (self hypnosis, meditation techniques, etc.). The Transcendental Meditation technique of Maharishi AyurVeda would be in this category.

The Patient's Capacity for Insight

A renowned psychiatrist, Peter Sifneos, MD, has promoted the term "alexithymia" in referring to patients who have little capacity for insight.[3] These individuals typically do poorly with "in-depth, insight-oriented psychotherapy." Usually a more supportive, concrete, behavioral or biological approach works best with these patients. I've found that there is a spectrum of alexithymia, in that people have a greater or lesser ability to look within themselves, which is often the first step in taking responsibility for their own actions. In my own clinical practice, in which I frequently recommend the Transcendental Meditation technique, *Panchakarma* (Ayurvedic purification therapy for the physiology), music therapy, and so on, I've found that patients can, believe it or not, go through a metamorphosis with regard to their capacity for insight. When people begin to transcend regularly, they experience inner peace, a state of mind devoid of fear. This allows them to be less afraid to face their own weaknesses, and enables them to begin to deal with their weaknesses in a constructive manner during the therapy process.

"June" was a lady in her mid-thirties who, when I first saw her, was feeling betrayed by two people in her life, her boyfriend and her roommate. She talked about how her boyfriend had gone to visit his hometown, where his old girlfriend still lived. She was furious with him, because she was "sure" he was going to look her up. In addition, she was angry with her roommate because she was spending more and more time with a man she had only recently met. I must admit that I began to feel some frustration with this patient because after five sessions, she still saw the only solution as being outside of herself, that is, "it was up to them to change." She was very resistant to looking at the role that *she* might be playing in why she was feeling so depressed and miserable. Fortunately for "June," she was open to learning how to meditate, with the understanding that it might help relax her nerves (which she felt were shot because of the way others were treating her). Within a few weeks of meditation practice, I was amazed at the change in her attitude towards therapy. She started looking at herself more objectively, and was less afraid to look at her own defenses (including the tendency to blame), which were covering up some deep wounds from the past. She felt more inner strength from her meditation, and therefore was better able to tolerate the uncomfortable feelings that she was harboring inside. "June" described how her hurts used to be too overshadowing to face — she felt "consumed" by them. After learning to meditate she began to feel that she herself was much greater than her problems, and hence they became manageable.

I have also found that even those very alexithymic patients who seem incapable of developing self-insight often start to feel better (less depressed or anxious) with the more behaviorally and biologically oriented techniques of Maharishi AyurVeda (meditation, daily oil massage, etc.). Most of my colleagues who are also trained in Ayurveda have had the same experience. For this reason I encourage my patients (if they are open to it) to avail themselves of Maharishi AyurVeda approaches *in conjunction* with the psychotherapy process. If we use the analogy of fine-tuning a violin, Maharishi AyurVeda is the tuner, and the therapy process is the instrument.

Maharishi AyurVeda and Therapy

Today, with the availability of Maharishi Ayur-Veda training programs for health professionals worldwide, many mental-health practitioners have integrated their knowledge from these courses into their counseling practice. I will discuss in this essay my own counseling experience and those of some of my colleagues. I will also share with you how one can apply Ayurvedic principles to counseling, regardless of one's particular training background. The information presented here comes from several sources, including classical Ayurvedic texts, knowledge learned from Ayurvedic physicians from India (called *Vaidyas*) with whom I have worked and studied,[4] Maharishi AyurVeda physician training courses, discussions with other psychiatrists trained in Maharishi

AyurVeda, and clinical experience.

Even though it's possible to clump the over a hundred types of therapy into three main groups, there still remain significant distinctions between each of them. Though each method is unique, is it possible to find some common, underlying principles that apply to all of them?

Ideal Therapist Qualities

In 1974 Dr. Hans Strupp found, through his research, that the specific type of therapy was not as important in the healing process as was what he called "non-specific factors."[5] He concluded that certain personality features of the patient and the therapist were helpful in promoting the healing. Important to the success of the therapy on the side of the therapist were empathy, compassion, confidence and expertise in one's technique, and concerned interest. On the side of the patient, receptivity, motivation, capacity for insight, and ability to accept responsibility were important.

These non-specific factors that have been found through research to be significant to the positive outcome of therapy are considered of great importance in Ayurveda. The Charaka Samhita[6] states that "to hold the honorable degree of *Vaidya*" (physician), he should "possess all the auspicious qualities like wisdom, practical knowledge, popularity, memory, devotion, experience, spiritual knowledge, intellect, friendliness, and compassion for the diseased." For a patient to have success in the healing process he or she should possess the qualities of "memory, obedience, fearlessness, and providing all information about the disorder."

It is also the common experience of many patients and therapists that there is more to the success of counseling than merely the particular "brand," whether it be transactional analysis, gestalt, psychoanalysis, or other therapies. Much like any relationship, there are three ingredients that must be considered: the behavior of the therapist, the behavior of the patient, and the interaction or "chemistry" between the two. As a practicing therapist for many years I've noticed that some patients, even though they may have the same diagnosis as other patients, don't seem to make much progress in spite of my best efforts. Yet other patients with the same diagnosis advance quickly toward recovery. Usually factors like motivation, receptivity, and capacity for insight seem to make a big difference in outcome.

I've also spoken with many patients who, in spite of their desire to get well, find that they just "can't relate" to their therapist. They find it difficult to form a trusting relationship because of a perceived lack of empathy or concerned interest from the side of the therapist. Unfortunately, training programs for therapists, whether they are for psychologists, psychiatrists, or social workers, are limited in their ability to teach these non-specific factors. Specific techniques and skills are taught, including how to be more empathic, but training-program directors are frequently frustrated because it is hard to teach someone how to be kind, compassionate, or even empathic. Unfortunately, with many of these qualities, it is thought that "you either have it, or you don't."

This is where Maharishi AyurVeda comes into play. Numerous studies have shown that regular practice of the Transcendental Meditation technique, for example, can help to develop certain personality characteristics that are usually considered "fixed" past a certain age. In particular, the non-specific qualities that are enhanced by Maharishi AyurVeda include friendliness, compassion, capacity for empathy, moral reasoning, intelligence, creativity, field independence (ability to see the whole picture while attending to the part), self-assuredness, and happiness.[7]

As a side note, I remember getting flack and suspicious remarks from some of my colleagues and professors during my psychiatry residency because I "smiled too much." This would especially occur at times of the day when most were tired and stressed, like early morning and late afternoon. What they didn't know was that these were the times when I had just finished meditating, so as a result I was feeling quite fresh, alert, and joyful. It was strange to me how seriousness and soberness (and perhaps even cynicism) was an unspoken requirement for being a "qualified" psychiatrist. Nonetheless, I've noticed that patients' moods would improve much more when I was in a good mood myself, and to the contrary they tended to be affected negatively when I wasn't in the best of humor. I felt quite reassured, and less like an anomaly, when I read Dr. Strupp's research, indicating that technical knowledge and skill are only part of what gets people better. A caring, concerned, interested demeanor, and yes, even feeling well and in good humor, can have a major impact on the overall healing process. Research (both by Strupp and studies showing the positive effects of Maharishi AyurVeda on personality development) supports the idea that training programs for mental-health professionals would be enhanced by including training in meditation and natural healing therapies that promote balanced mental health.

In the Ayurvedic literature there are many "case studies" of what is called the healing effects of "*Darshan*." *Darshan* is described as the "light" that a person radiates into the environment when he or she is a highly developed and mature person who is in constant contact with the unified field, or pure consciousness (hence the term "enlightenment"). It is said a person develops this natural state after many years of regular meditation, along with a healthy lifestyle (healthy diet, adequate rest and exercise, etc.). It is acknowledged, however, that some people are simply "genetically endowed" with high levels of enlightenment. These enlightened souls spontaneously radiate intense happiness, vibrant health, insight, intelligence, and compassion into their environment. Furthermore, just by one's proximity to such an individual, one begins to feel better.

The mechanics of how this *Darshan* works are better understood by looking at the human being in a "quantum mechanical" rather than a "Newtonian" way (Newton's physics sees the world as a series of "billiard balls," separated in time and space). From this quantum point of view, our nature is not just limited to our body, which seems to be sealed off from its environment. Since our deeper nature is pure consciousness (directly experienced during meditation that is done properly) and since pure consciousness is at the basis of everything in nature, we are all connected on this most subtle level. Pure consciousness is like a calm, quiet pond, and when a stone is thrown in a pond the ripples spread throughout. Similarly, when an individual has cultured his or her nervous system to the point where pure consciousness is very lively most or all of the time (leading to experiences of enlightenment), the individual spontaneously radiates this "inner light" out into the environment. There is a "tuning fork" effect with any person who happens to be nearby — that is, the pure consciousness in one person resonates with the pure consciousness in the other.

To make this a little more concrete, if we happen to enter a prison, the stress is quite palpable. (I know, because I have been in prison many times, not as an inmate, but as a Maharishi AyurVeda consultant to the prison.) Compare this "atmosphere" to that of a church, mosque, or synagogue, which on the contrary may feel very peaceful. This is the experience of the influence of group consciousness on the environment. It is not only a group of people who radiate their state of consciousness into their environment, but individuals do so, too. You may have had the experience of liking or disliking someone immediately, even before a word is spoken! As the therapist becomes more enlightened as a result of his or her spiritual development, just being in the presence of such an individual can have a healing effect on the patient over time. That's not to say that the therapist's technical skill, well-timed words, and empathy aren't important in the healing process, only that the more subtle, nonverbal processes that occur also have a powerful effect.

The renowned psychiatrist Harry Stack Sullivan described an important component of the healing that comes from the therapy relationship.[8] He said this was due to what he called a "corrective emotional experience." He postulated that disorders of various kinds, such as chronic depression and certain personality disorders, often arise due to a lack of development of certain parts of the ego. This gap in personality development occurs because something that should have occurred during the normal course of one's upbringing, particularly during early childhood, didn't happen. For example, if moral values are not instilled at an appropriate age, the person may be lacking in moral conscience, and may grow up with anti-social or criminal tendencies. Or, if a person doesn't have high self-esteem, it may be because during infancy and early childhood, when the caregiver should have provided an abundance of love and affection, this was not the case. There has been recent research indicating that there is an increase in depression in people whose mothers were depressed (and hence emotionally unavailable) during their infancy.

Most important in this regard is the development of "basic trust," which unfolds as a result of parental respect, kindness, unconditional acceptance, and love. During the course of their therapy with patients who initially lacked basic trust (and therefore had the associated low self-esteem) Sullivan and others found that it is possible to provide an environment conducive to attaining these developmental milestones. In my experience as a therapist, I've found that non-verbal (in addition to verbal) communication of love, concern, and respect for my patients consistently over time helps them acquire the capacity to trust and feel more self-secure. Of course, there are other benefits to be gained from the therapy relationship, such as self insight, getting in touch with and expressing one's feelings, reframing old outdated beliefs, and better coping skills. But promoting a corrective emotional experience through consistent guidance and support over time is of tremendous value in itself.

I have to say that I am quite aware that using a word like *love* in connection with counseling may seem to some in my field to be an inappropriate, if not a downright heretical, thing to say. (I also got some flack during my psychiatry training program for expressing ideas like this.) I think this is because society has cultured us to associate love with physical intimacy. Also, I think many consider that love does not have a place in the therapy setting because it's believed that feeling love indicates "over-involvement" with one's patient. Just to be clear, when I use this word I'm referring to the kind of love that is simple, spontaneous, and motivated not by one's own ego, but by a natural compassion, liking, and concern for a fellow human being. This is in keeping with how Maharishi AyurVeda can help both patient and therapist gain more advantage from the counseling experience. By adding the practice of Transcendental Meditation and other self-development strategies as an adjunct to the therapy process, the therapist naturally grows in the qualities of compassion, capacity for love, empathy, optimism, and greater appreciation for others. This allows patients to feel greater self-assuredness and an increased connectedness with others, which are ingredients necessary for the culturing of basic trust. It should be noted that Nancy McWilliams gives some good support to the importance of the therapist having a great capacity for love in the process of doing psychotherapy in her book *Psychoanalytic Psychotherapy*.[9]

Ayurvedic texts, in particular, emphasize three "ingredients" that promote psycho-physiological wellness in the psychotherapeutic relationship. These are encouragement, patience, and knowledge.

1. Encouragement

According to the Ayurvedic classics, the attitude of the physician toward the patient is considered very important to the healing process. Instilling hope and encouragement is especially emphasized. This does not mean that false hope should be given, but rather that a person cannot recover as effectively, no matter what the ailment, without hope. In the course of my medical training there have been several examples of patients who had "terminal" illnesses (various forms of malignant cancer, etc.) who ended up recovering despite the odds. One patient whom I remember had testicular cancer that had spread throughout his liver, bone, and lung. Despite the "grave" prognosis that he was given, he nonetheless recovered fully. What appeared to have contributed greatly to his recovery was the unending encouragement, support, and hope of his friends and family. This patient himself was "convinced" beyond a shadow of a doubt that he would recover. Fortunately the patient's physician, in spite of his own private skepticism, was always encouraging and instilling hope. I believe this greatly facilitated the healing process.

Unfortunately, this positive attitude is not always forthcoming on the part of the doctor. This has potentially harmful side effects for the patient. It is now known that the "placebo effect" is a very powerful force in the recovery process. Doctors used to consider the placebo effect to be equivalent to no effect, since it was the result of a "non-treatment" control group. It is now known that a typical placebo effect (where one is told one is getting an effective treatment but one isn't really) actually results in a 20–30% improvement anyway! Researchers have determined that even the *expectation* of benefit produces benefit. Studies have shown that when a person is given a placebo pill for pain it often works just like a narcotic, except that with the placebo the body produces its own natural narcotic in response to the expectation of relief! Research has also borne out that a negative expectation is likely to produce a negative outcome, due in part to the harmful chemicals produced in the body as a result.

Therefore, it is a scientific fact that encouragement and hope are necessary ingredients to the recovery process. In a counseling setting, this is especially important because emotional disorders like anxiety and depression can be very disabling, and are intrinsically associated with negativistic thinking. I've found that the difference between life and death (from suicide) in a depressed patient is often related to the counselor's frequent reminders that "it's only temporary, it'll soon be better" and "I'm here for you." Also, since most antidepressant medications take at least three weeks to work, what keeps these patients going during this long, tedious period are the words of hope and the frequent reminders to "hang in there" from the doctor. In this case, for three weeks the real and most helpful medicine is the *words* of the healer.

2. Patience

One of the hardest things for us to do is listen quietly to another person when they're talking to us, especially if it's for longer than one minute. On the other side, if we need to talk, and someone takes the time just to listen, it's incredible how powerfully healing this can be. When I studied Maharishi AyurVeda in India with Maharishi Mahesh Yogi, I asked him what the most important ingredient was for successful therapy. He thought for a minute, and then said, "patience, patience, patience." Since Maharishi was undoubtedly the most patient person I've ever known, I felt, at that moment, that he was revealing to me one of the secrets to his success as a great spiritual teacher.

3. Knowledge

Knowledge of the Patient's Psycho-physiological Style

For the therapist, an understanding of personality type is vital in working with clients. This can be determined through pulse diagnosis and by history and physical exam. This knowledge provides a way for the therapist to understand more about the people with whom he or she works. The patients also learn about themselves, and receive a master key to accepting and living with differences.

Many people have difficulty with the idea that they have a psychiatric diagnosis. It's a label that they feel brands them for life. It really can be a lifelong liability. Understanding one's difficulties in terms of physiological imbalances makes it much easier to accept one's condition, and also provides motivation to get well.

Ayurveda describes three basic governing aspects of the physiology, called *Doshas*. They are *Vata*, which refers to the nervous system; *Pitta*, which refers to metabolism; and *Kapha*, which refers to fluids and physical structure. I explain to my patients which *Doshas* are out of balance in their physiologies, giving rise to their conditions.

When one knows the nature of one's imbalance (e.g. *Vata*) then one can understand what the underlying causative or aggravating factors are (regarding diet, lifestyle, etc.). One can then take measures to reverse the disease process. This gives much more power and control over one's fate, as compared with the Western approach. (I am still advocating the use of the Western approach where appropriate, by the way.)

In my own practice, I'll usually tell the patient, "In Western terms, you would be labeled 'bipolar,' but from the Ayurvedic point of view, there is an alternating imbalance between two of the *Doshas*, *Vata* and *Kapha*" (leading to mania and depression). One manifestation of *Vata* imbalance is when there is too much *Vata*, which causes hyper-activity in the nervous system, or mania. When a person is depressed, it can be the result of excess *Kapha*, which can appear as sluggishness and lack of motivation.

Instead of understanding one's situation in terms of illness, one can grasp it as an imbalance. That is empowering to the patient. He or she can see the whole picture of what's going on in terms of the cause of the condition, what's going on in his or her body, and what to do about it. This is especially practical in terms of preventing relapse. Even genetic conditions like manic-depressive illness or schizophrenia are known to be stable at times, and aggravated at other times. So even if people have an illness that's more chronic, they gain a sense of empowerment — they can see that certain things in their lifestyles and behavior might contribute to the improvement of the condition, or, on the other hand, be responsible for the relapse. They begin to see that they have a genetic tendency toward some kind of imbalance, but with proper care of their mind and body, they can prevent recurrences, or at least make them less severe. In my experience with patients, being labeled tends to make a person feel helpless, just as hearing the word "cancer" promotes the feeling of giving up. On the other hand, learning about one's particular *Dosha* imbalance and what one can do to promote balance gives people the sense of hope. They become self-healers, to whatever extent, and this empowerment has a healing effect in itself.

I want to point out, however, that Ayurvedic approaches for more severe forms of mental imbalance do not usually preclude the use of allopathic medications. Ayurveda recognizes that they can be very helpful when used adjunctively.

One of my patients, "Michael," a 35-year-old man, was diagnosed as being a *Vata* type. He was tall and lanky, and was staying up late at night to work on a business project. After losing sleep and eating very little for a number of days, he developed a manic psychosis. "Michael," who had never experienced psychotic symptoms before, began hearing voices, thinking he was the Messiah, communicating with God and experiencing other symptoms. After he set himself on fire because he thought he was invincible, the authorities were called. When they arrived, "Michael" thought they were an alien force and became aggressive.

"Michael" took antipsychotic medication for a period of time, and eventually he was able to come off it. It was easy for him to see that staying up late and fasting, both of which aggravate *Vata*, would affect him adversely, since he had a *Vata* constitution to begin with. He simply slipped into a very *Vata*-aggravated condition, where his thinking was very scattered and his sense of reality was disturbed. The "*Akasha*" (space) element was increased. I explained to him that *Vata* consists of *Akasha* (space) and *Vayu* (motion). As the space element increased in his physiology, his sense of personal boundaries became blurred. He thought that people's thoughts were influencing him, and he became very fearful of others. It's as if the usual "psychological semi-permeable membrane" we all have, that filters out the things it's unnecessary for us to perceive, became disturbed because of the increased Akasha element. Thus, the distinction between himself and the environment became obscured or blurred. "Michael" understood this, and when he began to get enough sleep and do a few *Vata*-pacifying practices, he was quickly off the medications and he continued to do well. Of course, this individual may be susceptible under extreme stress to have a psychotic-type imbalance (just as someone else's "weak link" might be asthma, or a peptic ulcer). But he has learned how to modify his behavior in such a way as to prevent further recurrences. "Michael" greatly appreciated the knowledge and was motivated to assume responsibility, to whatever degree he could, for his health.

Application of Vedic Knowledge

When it comes to the application of Vedic knowledge to the therapy process, there are two elements to consider. The first and more important is experiential knowledge. This refers to the actual experience of one's inner unbounded awareness, or pure consciousness, during meditation and during other Maharishi AyurVeda approaches (like Gandharva Veda). This deepest aspect of one's Self provides the foundation for not only greater success in the counseling process, but even more importantly, for the daily nourishment of the mind, emotions, the five senses, and the physiology as a whole.

In addition to experiential knowledge, intellectual understanding is necessary. Understanding actually serves to enrich and enhance the quality of our experience. It helps us to appreciate the experiential techniques that we practice daily, and gives us inspiration to continue to be very regular in our practice as well. Therefore, intellectual knowledge is very helpful to the healing process.

When Vedic philosophy is added to counseling, there are various factors that are very helpful. These are not a part of the usual "Western" counseling format. I will give some examples of areas of Vedic knowledge that can be helpful in the therapeutic setting.

Knowledge of the Unified Field

Teaching patients about the underlying basis of life, described by quantum physics as the unified field, has a powerful healing influence. Knowledge of the unified field should be experiential (as it is during the practice of the Transcendental Meditation technique). This is ultimately necessary for complete healing. Yet even intellectual knowledge of the subject can be very helpful in the counseling setting. Learning about this deepest spiritual aspect of life, that underlies the mind and body, inspires people to be regular in their meditation practice and other aspects of their Ayurvedic routine. It also encourages them and gives them hope, knowing that at the very core of their existence lies the storehouse of infinite energy, wisdom, and happiness. Maharishi AyurVeda teaches that the key to removing any suffering in life comes from two angles: 1) removing the blocks that keep one from experiencing the unified field and 2) learning techniques that foster direct experience of it. It's a great relief to know that one has the innate ability to promote self-healing with just a little education and guidance.

Disease is understood in Maharishi AyurVeda to be a block in the flow between the underlying intelligence of the physiology and the more manifested aspects of it. Just as darkness begins to dissipate when a light is turned on, so the blocks in the channels of the physiology begin to dissipate as an individual contacts the unified field, or pure consciousness (this process is referred to as "transcending"). The result is a more balanced psychology and physiology. This understanding and experience motivates a person to practice his or her Ayurvedic techniques regularly. In my experience, a large proportion of the problems seen in clinical practice are significantly helped as a result of the patient learning a technique that enables them to transcend. This is especially true for problems like low-grade depression, insomnia, anxiety, and personality problems. Many people find, when they begin to have contact with inner peace during the transcending process, that personality tendencies like shyness, selfishness, and hostility tend to lessen greatly. A number of common problems seen by mental-health professionals can be corrected in a short time as a result of a few profound experiences of identifying one's Self as the unified field. The Upanishads, an aspect of the Vedic literature that discusses the importance of daily contact with the unified field, describe this "aha" experience in the expression "*Aham Brahmasmi*," which means "I am infinite."

Knowledge of Stress and Its Release

There is extensive published scientific research on the Transcendental Meditation technique as an effective method for releasing stress. This technique has been shown to be effective in treatment of many stress-related psychological and medical disorders. These include hypertension, heart disease, high cholesterol, asthma, anxiety, depression, and post-traumatic stress disorder, including in the treatment of combat veterans.[10]

According to Maharishi AyurVeda, stress resulting from past unpleasant or unhealthy experiences becomes lodged in the hardware of the nervous system, and in other locations in the body. Natural physiological mechanisms work to re-balance the body and counteract the effects of stress. Rest is a great natural antidote to stress, widely recommended medically. Because the Transcendental Meditation technique provides a profound level of rest, deep-rooted stresses can be dissolved naturally during and as a result of practicing this technique. When people learn Transcendental Meditation, their teacher also gives them an understanding — based on direct experience — of ways in which the natural process of stress release affects mind and body.

Understanding stress and its effects can be helpful in a therapeutic setting. Stress and the body's natural processes to recover from it and regain balance — or homeostasis — affect the mind. Recognizing this can trigger a process of "cognitive restructuring" which helps relieve gripping mental experiences caused by stress, and gives practical knowledge for effective stress management. Can you imagine the relief a person with a lot of anger feels when he or she realizes that when anger rises it is not due to their being a "bad" person? Instead it may be due to the intelligence of the body, attempting to purify itself of stress caused by some past negative influence. This information must, of course, be coupled with practical techniques that don't suppress the anger, but rather help the body to release it safely, comfortably, and more effectively, such as the Transcendental Meditation technique.

It is important to point out that there are also some psychotherapies that help a person release deeply repressed emotions in a safe and efficient manner. This way of releasing "deep rooted stresses" also has the effect of reducing the grip that those stresses previously had on the person's overall personality. This is an example of how techniques of Maharishi AyurVeda and modern psychotherapy methods can be complementary to each other.

After a while, people can become quite adept at gaining some distance from their worries and feelings of frustration. In psychiatry jargon this is called developing the "observing ego." What begins to happen is that when some irritating thought comes up in the mind (usually directed at someone close to them) the individual recognizes what is happening. The thought arises, "don't act on these thoughts; after all, they are only an indication of my body attempting to process some stress from past experience." With this understanding the person has created a gap between the thought and the behavior, which is helpful in managing stress (though understanding alone doesn't release the physical stress). As a result he or she now has time to choose a different type of behavior, instead of saying something mean or hurtful to a friend or loved one. He or she is then in a position to choose an alternative behavior, like engaging in some pleasant activity, such as listening to music, exercising, talking with a trusted friend (to get it off their chest), closing the eyes for a few minutes, or just letting the feeling pass, as it usually does, if one has the patience to ride it out.

Psychotherapeutic Use of Vedic Literature

In Maharishi AyurVeda there are three basic components to the healing process in the counseling setting. They are known in the Sanskrit language as Rishi, Devata, and Chhandas. The English translation for these three is knower, process of knowing, and known.

The knower represents the therapist. In ancient times the therapist was not called a "mental-health professional," but was usually either the family physician (a *Vaidya*) or the person's *Guru* or sage. He or she represented the source of wisdom, inspiration, and healing.

The known value is the object or receiver of knowledge, the patient or seeker.

The process of knowing refers to the dynamic interaction between sage and seeker. In the Vedic literature, the result of this interaction has not only the potential for the restoration of health and happiness, but also for higher stages of human development — enlightenment.

Another way to see the therapy process is from the viewpoint of the patient. The patient develops as a knower as his or her way of experiencing and interpreting (process of knowing) surroundings and circumstances (known) changes and develops.

There are many "case studies" in the Vedic literature that depict the process of what we now call psychotherapy. I have found not only that the study of these interactions is helpful in refining my psychotherapy skills, but that sharing these stories with patients often provides them with knowledge and inspiration that can enhance the healing process.

Ayurveda and Psychotherapy

One case study, over 5000 years old, is found in a book called the Yoga Vasishta.[11] This is the story of Rama, a young prince, who presents with classical symptoms of depression: "He is bereft of hope, he is bereft of desire." To the modern mental-health professional reading this, Rama looks as if he is overwhelmed by suicidal thoughts spurred by the feelings of despondency. Rama describes that he is depressed because he saw that life is not permanent, everything is of a fleeting nature. Rama says, "What do people call happiness and can it be had in the ever-changing objects of this world? All beings in this world take birth but to die, and they die to be born! I do not perceive any meaning in all these transient phenomena, which are the roots of suffering and sin. Unrelated beings come together; the mind conjures up a relationship between them. Everything in this world is dependent upon the mind, upon one's mental attitude. On examination, the mind itself appears to be unreal! But we are bewitched by it. We seem to be running after a mirage in the desert to slake our thirst … my heart bleeds with sorrow."

His sage and mentor, Vasishta, counsels Rama, and through what appears to be what we would today call "brief psychotherapy," Rama is cured. Vasishta uses the three pillars of counseling — encouragement, patience, and knowledge — to help Rama out of his predicament.

Earlier in this essay these three same qualities were discussed in terms of modern scientific research and the Vedic texts in general. Below are actual case studies from the Yoga Vasishta and other branches of Vedic literature where the three important qualities of the therapist previously mentioned are exemplified.

1. Encouragement

Vasishta gives Rama hope by inspiring him to see that there is a way out of his dilemma. He gives him a vision of all the possibilities that are in store for him once he gets through his existential crisis. Vasishta really goes all out in revealing to Rama how good life could be if he were to follow Vasistha's guidance. "O Rama, if you thus overcome this sorrow of repetitive history, you will live here on earth itself like a god, like Brahma or Vishnu! For when delusion is gone and the truth is realized by means of inquiry into self-nature, when the mind is at peace and the heart leaps to the supreme truth, when all the disturbing thought waves in the mind-stuff have subsided and there is unbroken flow of peace and the heart is filled with the bliss of the absolute, when thus the truth has been seen in the heart, then this very world becomes an abode of bliss."

2. Patience

Vasishta spends a long time listening to the litany of Rama's woes. It makes one want to scream just listening to it! But Vasishta's patience enables Rama to trust him, in addition to helping him get a lot off his chest.

3. Knowledge

Vasishta gives Rama both intellectual and practical knowledge, essentially teaching him Maharishi AyurVeda in a nutshell. Rama learns that by shifting his attention from the transitory world of objects to the inner aspect of life, the Self, he will gain inner peace and contentment, and will begin to see life with a broader and more balanced perspective. "O Rama, thus do inquire into the nature of the Self ... where the mental activity has come to a standstill. You are the knower of all — the Self. You are the unborn being, you are the supreme Lord; you are non-different from the Self which pervades everything. He who has abandoned the idea that there is an object of perception which is other than the Self is not subjected to the defects born of joy and grief. He is known as a Yogi. He who is confirmed in his conviction that the infinite consciousness alone exists, is instantly freed from the ... twin urges of acquisition and rejection ... and has reached the state of utter tranquility."

There are numerous other accounts in the Vedic literature which, when studied and utilized in the counseling session as a teaching guide, can be profoundly helpful. This is especially so for the Bhagavad-Gita ("Song of God"), to which I have devoted a whole essay (see Essay 4 on the Bhagavad-Gita).

One recent patient of mine, "Marge," was suffering from severe depression related to her husband's death. She saw no reason to live, and wanted to be reunited with him. I shared with her some quotes from the Bhagavad-Gita. She also learned the Transcendental Meditation technique, which is the meditation technique recommended in Chapter 2 of the Bhagavad-Gita. This book contains helpful knowledge for people suffering from grief associated with major loss. It helps provide the perspective that at a deep level we are all connected. The Bhagavad-Gita teaches that by contacting the unified field that lies inside us all (during meditation), we can transcend the field of grief and suffering. These are always born out of the sense of separation, disconnectedness, and loss. In hearing about the eternal, invincible nature of our inner selves, we are inspired to rise above our grief and depression. In learning and experiencing this wisdom from the Bhagavad-Gita, "Marge" came to a point by the end of her therapy where she was feeling a great sense of peace and tranquility, more than she had ever felt before in her life. I will end by sharing with you some of "Marge's" favorite quotes from the Bhagavad-Gita. Along with her recently learned meditation practice, she found these verses particularly helpful in overcoming her grief.

*As a man casting off worn-out garments
takes other new ones, so the dweller
in the body casting off worn-out
bodies takes others that are new.*

*Weapons cannot cleave him, nor fire
burn him; water cannot wet him, nor
wind dry him away.*

*He is uncleavable; he cannot be burned;
he cannot be wetted, nor yet can he be
dried. He is eternal, all-pervading,
stable, immovable, ever the same.*

*He is declared to be unmanifest,
unthinkable, unchangeable; therefore
knowing him as such you should not grieve.*
(Bhagavad-Gita, II, 22–25)

*Certain indeed is death for the born
and certain is birth for the dead;
therefore over the inevitable you
should not grieve.*

> *Creatures are unmanifest in the beginning, manifest in the middle state and unmanifest again at the end, O Bharata! What grief is there in this?*
> (Bhagavad-Gita, II, 27–28)

> *He who dwells in the body of everyone is eternal and invulnerable, O Bharata; therefore you should not grieve for any creature whatsoever.*
> (Bhagavad-Gita, II, 30)

> *Be ... freed from duality, ever firm in purity, independent of possessions, possessed of the Self.*
> (Bhagavad-Gita, II, 45)

> *Established in Yoga, O winner of wealth, perform actions having abandoned attachment and having become balanced in success and failure, for balance of mind is called Yoga.*
> (Bhagavad-Gita, II, 48)[12]

Notes

1. Morris B. Parloff, *Handbook of Psychotherapy and Behavioral Change* (1978).
2. T. Byram Karasu, *American Journal of Psychiatry* (August 1977).
3. Peter Sifneos, *Psychotherapy and Psychosomatics* 22, no. 2 (1973), 255–262.
4. Drs. Kasture, Kartikar, Subedhar, Triguna, Raju, Balraj Maharishi, Manohar, Nanal, and Desai.
5. Hans Strupp, in *Psychosomatics* (1974, footnote).
6. From chapter on Sutrasthana (Fundamentals) in *Caraka-Samhita Chaukhambha Orientalis, Vols. 1 and 2*, Prof. Priyavrat Sharma (Ed.) (Varanasi & Delhi: Jaikrishnadas Ayurveda Series No. 36).
7. *International Journal of Neuroscience*, no. 13 (1981), 211–217; no. 15 (1981), 151–157.
8. Harry Stack Sullivan, *The Interpersonal Theory of Psychiatry* (NY, USA: W.W. Norton & Co., 1953).
9. Nancy McWilliams, *Psychoanalytic Psychotherapy, A Practitioner's Guide* (Gulford Press, 2004).
10. D.W. Orme-Johnson, J.T. Farrow (Eds.), *Scientific Research on the Transcendental Meditation Program: Collected Papers, Vol. 1* (Livingston Manor, New York: Maharishi International University Press, 1977).

    R. Chalmers, G. Clements, H. Schenkluhn, M. Weinless (Eds.), *Scientific Research on Maharishi's Transcendental Meditation and TM-Sidhi Programme: Collected Papers, Vols. 2–4* (The Netherlands: Maharishi Vedic University Press, 1989).

R.K. Wallace, D.W. Orme-Johnson, M.C. Dillbeck (Eds.) *Scientific Research on Maharishi's Transcendental Meditation and TM-Sidhi Program: Collected Papers, Vol. 5* (Iowa, USA: Maharishi International University Press, 1990).

M.C. Dillbeck (Ed.) *Scientific Research on Maharishi's Transcendental Meditation and TM-Sidhi Programme: Collected Papers, Vol. 6* (The Netherlands: Maharishi Vedic University Press, 2011).

M.C. Dillbeck, V.A. Barnes, R.H. Schneider, F.T. Travis, K.G. Walton (Eds.) *Scientific Research on the Transcendental Meditation and TM-Sidhi Programme: Collected Papers, Vol. 7* (The Netherlands: Maharishi Vedic University Press, 2013).

J. Brooks and T. Scarano, "TM in the Treatment of Post Vietnam Adjustment." *The Journal of Counseling and Development* 64 (1985), 212–215.

B. Rees, F. Travis, D. Shapiro, R. Chant, "Reduction in Post-traumatic Stress Symptoms in Congolese Refugees Practicing Transcendental Meditation." *Journal of Traumatic Stress* 26, no. 2 (2013), 295–298.

11. Swami Venkatesananda, *Yoga Vasishta* (State University of New York Press, Albany, 1993).

12. All Bhagavad-Gita quotes are from *Maharishi Mahesh Yogi on the Bhagavad-Gita, A New Translation and Commentary, Chapters 1–6* (Penguin Books, 1967/1990).

REFLECTIONS ON
MAHARISHI AYURVEDA
AND MENTAL HEALTH

ESSAY 3

Sattwa Vijaya:
A Balanced Mind
Is Victorious

ESSAY 3

Sattwa Vijaya: A Balanced Mind Is Victorious

I have titled this essay *Sattwa Vijaya*, a term for mental health used in the Ayurvedic text Charaka and other Vedic texts. This name emphasizes the importance of culturing a fully balanced mind, or "enlightenment," as an antidote for mental and emotional imbalances.

In the classical texts of Ayurveda, however, the most common term used for psychiatry is *"Bhut Vidya."* It is one of the eight main branches of Ayurveda:

- Internal Medicine — *Kayachikitsa*
- Ears, Nose, and Throat — *Shalakya Tantra*
- Toxicology — *Vishagara Vairodh Tantra*
- Pediatrics — *Kaumara Bhritya*
- Surgery — *Shalya Tantra*
- Psychiatry — *Bhut Vidya*

- Aphrodisiacs — *Vajikarana*
- Longevity/Rejuvenation — *Rasayana*

Bhut Vidya is sometimes translated as "knowledge of ghosts." This translation hardly does justice to the deeper meaning of the name. *Bhut* means ghosts, and in part is in reference to the hallucinations experienced in more severe forms of mental illness like schizophrenia. In the field of mental health it also refers to unreal, unclear, or incomplete thinking or perception. Hence Ayurvedic Psychiatry refers to how to gain knowledge of seeing and understanding oneself and one's surroundings more clearly and accurately. Also, *Bhut* relates to the Ayurvedic term *Mahabhutas*, which refers to the underlying five elements, the ingredients that combine to form everything existent in nature. Hence, *Bhut Vidya* refers to gaining knowledge and mastery of the laws of nature.

In this essay I will briefly explain the causes of mental and emotional imbalance and disorders as understood by Ayurveda, and then I will outline the fundamental treatment modalities taught in the classical Ayurvedic texts, such as the Charaka Samhita.

Origins of Mental and Emotional Imbalance

Thousands of years before the advent of the environmental movement, Ayurveda taught that nature is an interrelated whole, and that human beings are part of that whole, inseparably part of the natural world in the living, intelligent, self-regulatory entirety. Our health and well-being depend on that connection.

Nature is upheld by laws and patterns that govern all growth and interaction. In the physical world, such phenomena as gravity and the laws of thermodynamics regulate the interactions of matter. Planets and galaxies revolve in harmony with each other. Day follows night. In all living things, growth follows a predictable sequence. Seeds split open, sprout roots and stems, and grow into tall trees in orderly progression.

In our individual lives, laws of nature also operate actively. Pure, fresh food is nourishing to body and mind; if we ignore that law and eat stale, heavy food, we pay the price. Kind words and generous deeds bring love and kindness in return; sharp words and cruel actions elicit unhappiness and resentment. Rest is the basis of activity; if we try to go without rest, we pay the price in reduced alertness and effectiveness; if we push it too far, our health collapses. Like trying to swim upstream, violation of natural laws results in struggle and suffering; attunement with them results in health, happiness and growth.

In short, life in harmony with nature and the laws of nature is a healthy life. Violation of natural law is the cause of discomfort and disease. To treat and prevent disease as well as to enjoy a more ideal state of health, we need to align ourselves with nature.

There are two basic ways to accomplish this alignment. The first is to set up our outward behavior to correspond to natural rhythms and laws: to rise with the sun and go to sleep at sundown, to eat local food that is nourishing and avoid what is unhealthy, to make use of the healing and strengthening herbs that have been placed by nature all over the earth, and so on.

The second way to align ourselves with natural law is inward, and is the more direct path, though one that is commonly overlooked. According to ancient Vedic wisdom, the Self is the seat of nature's intelligence. According to Ayurveda, as explained by the great Vedic scholar Maharishi Mahesh Yogi (whose modern interpretation of Ayurveda is called "Maharishi AyurVeda"), the entire creation sprouts from the Self, the unified field of natural law. Inherent in the silence of the Self are the intelligent laws that govern the unfoldment of creation and regulate all the levels of dynamism in the natural world.

Sattwa Vijaya: A Balanced Mind Is Victorious

The process described by Maharishi as gaining self-referral consciousness, or transcendence, occurs regularly during the practice of the Transcendental Meditation technique, and puts us in touch with that all-encompassing intelligence.[1] It enlivens the innate, self-regulating intelligence of the body and brings healing and wholeness.

The great Ayurvedic physician Maharishi Charaka states in the Charaka Samhita that the main cause of disease is *Pragyaparadha*, the "mistake of the intellect." The intellect has a decision-making role in our lives. Charaka goes on to explain that decisions that give rise to actions contrary to nature are made either knowingly or unknowingly.

Some examples of decisions made knowingly are: eating a whole large pizza and two desserts, staying up all night, and excess stimulation (overdoing it in any field of activity including eating, sex, exercise). Basically, the concept of *decisions contrary to nature* refers to any decision that leads to action that produces health problems for the body and dullness or agitation for the mind. Charaka clearly states (C.S. VI, 9, 4–5): "The causes of mental imbalance include, amongst other things, wrong food (either spoiled, or unsuitable for one's constitutional type), and violation of natural law such as negative behavior toward others."[2]

The definition of *Pragyaparadha* in Maharishi Ayur-

Veda includes an even deeper level of consideration. Maharishi describes Ayurveda as dealing "with the intellect, which is the main controller and administrator of all activity."[3] The intellect is defined as the very subtle deciding faculty of the psyche. It lies deeper than the mind, the function of which is to think. This distinction is important. Using the process of thinking we can enumerate, classify, and mull over alternatives forever. A deeper aspect of our nature ultimately chooses one of the alternatives. That is the intellect. (In Maharishi AyurVeda the word "mind" is used in two ways: as here, indicating the active thinking function, and also as inclusive of all levels of thinking, feeling, deciding.)

The Self, as defined in Maharishi AyurVeda, is pure unbounded awareness, pure intelligence. The intellect, operating at the finest level of individual consciousness, stands between the unboundedness of the Self and the boundaries of thought, perception, and action (see diagram).

When the intellect is directed only outward, it tends to be unsteady or wavering, but with repeated experience of transcending a state of "steady intellect" is gained.[4] In this state, individual awareness naturally maintains experience of the Self and is balanced through all activity of the mind and sense perceptions, through all the plans, cares, charms, or problems of life.

Sattwa Vijaya: A Balanced Mind Is Victorious

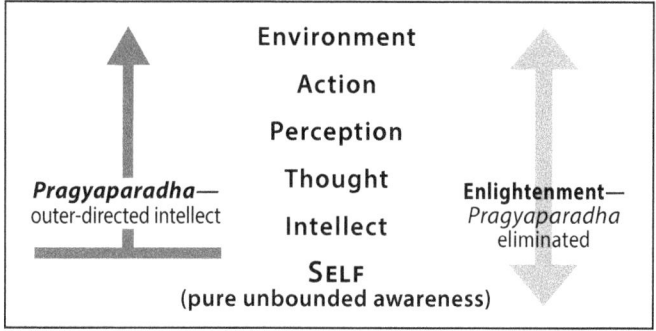

There is a parallel to this in the branch of the Vedic literature called *Nyaya*, which Maharishi describes as having a "distinguishing and deciding" quality of intelligence and as being "the lamp at the door," capable of lighting both inner and outer values of "the house" (individual awareness) — the inner Self and the outer experience of thoughts, emotions, and actions. When individual awareness is fully developed, this "distinguishing and deciding" quality naturally balances inner and outer.

Pragyaparadha means that the intellect is caught up in the ever-changing boundaries, and forgets about the Self, the underlying, unbounded reality that is the inner source of intelligence, creativity, peace, and joy. It causes us to identify ourselves in terms of boundaries, to believe that we are time–space bound beings, when the truth is that — although we are indeed operating in time and space — our deepest and truest nature lies beyond the field of boundaries. When *Pragyaparadha* is eliminated and we experience our identity as the Self, the result is self-esteem, happiness, stability, and inner peace.

Thus the mistake of the intellect, or false belief, comes from the failure to know the deepest truth about oneself and about life. When we are so caught up in boundaries that the Self is forgotten, we actually experience being cut off from our own Self or wholeness. *Pragyaparadha* means that we are not consciously connected to our Self, which by nature is fullness and bliss.

It also means that we are disconnected from the intelligence that underlies all the expressions of natural law. When we are consciously connected to that level of life, we spontaneously start operating with the full support of all the laws of nature. By being out of touch with our Self, we are cut off from the innocent and spontaneous right-doing, the freely chosen healthy decisions and actions that characterize ideal behavior. When we are cut off from that pure intelligence, violation of natural law becomes inevitable, and imbalance and illness can follow.

Pragyaparadha refers to those "wrong" (that is, unhealthy) choices leading to actions that take us out of alignment with what's beneficial to our own nature. Medical and mental-health professionals often offer clients dozens of suggestions for altering diet, daily routine, and lifestyle in order to help them achieve that attunement, such as "stop smoking, stop drinking, go to bed earlier."

The deeper way to address *Pragyaparadha*, however, is to transcend the field of relative knowledge and information entirely, and experience the Self, the field of pure consciousness. This in itself puts us in harmony with nature, the universe, and the divine.

The main goal of Ayurveda is to function in harmony with nature. The cause of *Pragyaparadha* lies in not being in harmony with nature. The antidote to *Pragyaparadha* lies in restoring that harmony. The key to that is experience of self-referral consciousness.

Ayurvedic (*Sattwa Vijaya*) Treatment Modalities for Mental Health

When imbalance (due to *Pragyaparadha*) has been created, treatment is required. The methods of treatment can be divided into four major categories. The first three correspond to Western methods — psychological, physiological, and behavioral — although they often differ significantly from the Western approaches under these categories. The fourth category embraces the spiritual or quantum mechanical dimension.

I cannot emphasize strongly enough that these

approaches are not intended strictly for therapeutic purposes once problems arise. They can be used — and are highly recommended — for prevention, in order to maintain a state of optimum health. Thus, every time I use the word "patient," you might also read, "the student of Ayurveda," or "the seeker of knowledge." Actually, in the classical Ayurvedic texts, the term used instead of patient is "*purusha.*" *Purusha* also refers to the silence of the "Self," the deepest aspect of a human being, which is eternal, blissful, and immortal — the spiritual aspect of our being. How refreshing it would be if one day medical doctors viewed their patients and addressed them at the level of their true essence, from the level of wholeness and perfect health!

Psychological Approach of *Sattwa Vijaya*

This category of treatment integrates four elements:

1. Knowledge and understanding: the cognitive component — *Gyan*
2. The role of memory — *Smriti*
3. Patience, empathy, compassion, and encouragement: the supportive component — *Dhairya*
4. Self-referral consciousness — *Samadhi*

Sattwa Vijaya: A Balanced Mind Is Victorious

1. The Role of Knowledge (*Gyan*)

The cognitive or intellectual component of Ayurveda ranges from knowledge of one's personal situation to the highest Self-knowledge (*Atma-Gyan*). It includes:
- knowledge about one's personality, family, abilities and failings, past history, etc.;
- knowledge about life, its structure and ultimate aim;
- knowledge about what the Self is and how it can be developed;
- knowledge of the laws of nature having to do with human behavior and the guidelines for evolutionary behavior (known in Sanskrit as *Sadvritta* or Behavioral Rasayanas);
- knowledge of the constitutional types, knowing one's own type, and how to regulate one's diet, routine, etc. in such a way that one's own constitution thrives; and
- understanding of actions and their consequences (*Karma*), such as the effects of right and wrong diet, and proper, excess, or insufficient exercise.

This cognitive approach gives much to the patient. One gains:
- concrete skills to intelligently regulate one's life;
- inspiration and hope, due to having a more clear

and bright vision of the possibilities for this life;
- an increased sense of responsibility for oneself and control over one's life;
- an increased ability to stand back and observe oneself, and to see the transitory nature of the moment in the context of the larger picture of one's life; and
- an understanding that one's nature is, at its essence, spiritual, inspiring one to restructure priorities to include time for spiritual development.

2. Importance of Memory (*Smriti*)

Psychotherapeutic techniques since the time of Freud have emphasized the need for releasing painful stored memories, said to be the source of those present-day patterns of thinking, feeling, and acting that are unproductive for the individual. Getting in touch with past memories, processing them, and releasing them constitutes one of psychology's primary goals for promoting more ideal mental health.

Ayurveda also recognizes the importance of freeing oneself from the stressful impressions of the past. However, one important difference between modern psychotherapy and Maharishi AyurVeda is that the latter aims to make the process of stress release easy and comfortable, so that the individual does not incur additional stress and fatigue through the process of intense releasing. This elimination of the stresses of the past is achieved efficiently through various Ayurvedic techniques that gently dissolve the deep-rooted impressions, without the necessity of dealing with their specific, often painful contents. (Of course, practically speaking, effective and evidenced-based techniques of modern psychotherapy can often be extremely helpful when used in a complementary way with Maharishi AyurVeda. For example, if deep inner emotional work that involves freeing oneself from deep-seated, false beliefs is indicated, practicing the Transcendental Meditation technique afterwards can eliminate the fatigue from the intense, hard emotional work that was done prior.)

Ayurveda also deals with the subject of memory (*Smriti*) in an entirely different way. Vedic wisdom holds that there is one vital memory that everyone has lost, the restoration of which totally transforms one's life: that is memory of the Self. This area of one's being lies below the subconscious part of the mind that houses past traumas, at the deepest level of our existence. It is a field free of stress and trauma, the content of which is unlimited creative intelligence and bliss. An important focus of the Ayurvedic approach to therapy is to help the individual restore this lost memory, both by informing him about it (the cognitive component) and by teaching him techniques to directly experience it (*Samadhi* or self-referral consciousness, effectively accomplished during the practice of the Transcendental Meditation technique).

3. Supportive Component (*Dhairya*)

Ayurvedic counseling, not unlike modern psychotherapy, offers empathy, support, and patience to provide an environment conducive to a person's healing and learning. The client learns to trust the therapist due to the therapist's qualities of patience and empathy, being a good listener, and being accepting. That trust itself is healing to the patient, and allows him or her to feel comfortable exploring and expressing feelings.

Through the example of the therapist, patients also develop patience and self-acceptance. They gain a greater degree of control over their impulses, cravings, obsessions, passions, and grief by stepping quietly aside from themselves, observing their feelings, and attempting to discuss and understand them rather than being totally caught up in them. In this way, they develop self-understanding via the role modeling of the therapist.

Compassion and empathy are emphasized in the training of Western therapists, whether psychiatrists, social workers, or psychologists. However, this is one of the most difficult areas of the training process, since one is not taught how to become more compassionate. To a large extent, this is considered to be a quality that one either has or does not have.

Maharishi AyurVeda, with its proven methodologies for stress reduction, refinement of feelings, and self-actualization, can, in my opinion, serve a major role in the training of therapists. Because modern research indicates that successful therapy depends as much on the personality style of the patient as it does on that of the therapist, techniques for enhancing personality development are equally valuable for both patient and therapist.

In the following section, the principal technique for bringing out these humane qualities is described.

4. Self-referral Consciousness (*Samadhi*)

Charaka (I, 1, 58) cites experience of *Samadhi* as one of the major techniques to heal mental illness and create a state of mental and emotional health. *Samadhi* can be translated as transcendence, self-referral pure consciousness, or unbounded awareness. It is an experience of inner silence and freedom from boundaries that produces a transformation of character and personality, as well as conferring what Vedic knowledge defines as the ultimate goal of life, liberation or enlightenment.

The experience of *Samadhi* significantly enhances all

three above-mentioned components of therapy (*Gyan*, *Smriti*, and *Dhairya*). In terms of *Gyan*, the experience of self-referral consciousness provides a level of direct knowledge that simply cannot be attained through books or through the intellect. One gains from this experience not only a profound sense of Self-knowing and experience of a higher level of consciousness, but also a truer perception of the world.

Through knowledge of one's own nature, which is part of nature as a whole, one gains an intimate knowledge of natural law. This direct inner experience imparts a more personally relevant meaning to the principles offered in the therapeutic setting.

Experience of *Samadhi* is the process by which we return to ourselves. This is the most profound level of *Smriti*, or remembering.

Dhairya, or support, is often thought of as a quality that we "lend" to others to help them in their time of need. However, experience of *Samadhi* is perhaps the ultimate way of giving support to ourselves. In addition, when we experience the Self, our awareness is stationed where all the laws of nature are lively in our awareness. As a result we are able to receive the support of all the laws of nature in that place.

The value of *Samadhi* for developing patience and

compassion is manifold. Unbounded awareness results in a much broader comprehension of the situation one is dealing with in daily life. One has a stable base of inner quietness that allows for a clearer, more objective view. One's vision is less clouded by emotions and illusions. As stated in the Tao Te Ching, "The truth is seen only by eyes unclouded by longing." Events that can ordinarily be disquieting or worse simply don't upset one.

For example, the technology of transcending is beneficial to a therapist if a client gets angry with him or her. If the therapist is experienced in the daily practice of *Samadhi*, it becomes much easier to see that the client is upset by something, and is out of balance and out of control. The therapist who has more of a natural witnessing and observing capability is much less likely to take it personally. This enables the therapist to stay present to the client, and makes it less likely for his or her own reactions or agendas to infect the therapy process. (In psychoanalytic terms, the therapist is less affected by and is more aware of his or her counter-transference.)

In addition, the therapist who regularly experiences unbounded awareness develops increasing levels of patience. With a quiet mind and balanced emotions, he or she can listen empathically and insightfully to the patient's story, and discriminate the best path of action to take in every situation. The very presence of such a settled, self-possessed therapist is healing. This is what some Eastern traditions speak of as "*Darshan*," or presence. It is said that just being in the presence of a saint brings spiritual illumination. Therapists who develop self-referral consciousness through their spiritual practice spontaneously put patients at ease and help them feel free to be themselves. Patients feel uplifted and accepted.

For patients, *Samadhi* is the best prescription for numerous emotional disorders and imbalances, such as cravings and addictions, grief, anger, envy, greed, and fear. As the experience of pure consciousness becomes stabilized in one's awareness (with the regular practice of Transcendental Meditation) the Self, the silent witness of all activity, becomes permanently present through all the changes of day and night. As Maharishi comments, "The Self, in its real nature, is only the silent witness of everything."[5] This allows one to be non-attached and steady within the Self in all situations. Deep within, one's consciousness remains serene and secure. Whatever comes up, one remains fulfilled. One doesn't get caught up in the particular fluctuations of consciousness that belong to the moment. Of course, this doesn't happen all at once, but with regular diving into that unbounded ocean of consciousness, the ability to maintain evenness in the face of

Sattwa Vijaya: A Balanced Mind Is Victorious

adversity or conflict gradually develops over time.

One example of this is in the area of addiction treatment. I once gave a workshop to a group of substance abusers who were actively involved in Alcoholics Anonymous (AA) and Narcotics Anonymous (NA). They had all adopted the Transcendental Meditation technique as an adjunct to their regular AA/NA 12-step program. They explained to me that by meditating regularly (20 minutes twice per day) they found that when the urges to use came up, they didn't feel so pulled in to following those urges. Rather, they described how they experienced a type of "witnessing value." They still had urges, but at the same time, they also felt calm and content inside themselves. Therefore, they were much more able to watch the urges as if from a distance, and with this added perspective, were much more able to control the urges.

It is like throwing a rock into the ocean. The little ripples don't disturb the unbounded grandeur of the sea. The vastness and integrity aren't affected at all. The Self is like the ocean, and when established in one's awareness, no matter what fluctuations occur from one's daily experiences, it maintains its integrity. Brain research on the Transcendental Meditation technique demonstrates how this occurs from a neurophysiological perspective. Initially, researchers have identified a pattern of brain coherence, during the practice of meditation, not seen in other practices or mental states. Furthermore, studies show that this type of coherence (different parts of the brain operating in synchrony with each other) is associated with greater emotional stability and maturity in the practitioner. Over time, the brain of a person who is practicing transcending on a regular basis begins to function with this same level of coherence even while engaged in activity. Hence, the regular practitioner of the Transcendental Meditation technique increasingly becomes able to stay calm and emotionally stable in the face of any type of adversity.

When we are shaken by emotions and lose the integrity of our Self, our vision gets clouded over. We lose the ability to see clearly and understand properly, and we are prone to making poor choices. This is like the effect of a stone thrown into a puddle or a small pond. The mud is stirred up from the bottom, and the turbulence overtakes the whole pond.

This is what happens in the mind when the Self (associated physiologically with a high level of brain coherence) is lost to awareness. The experiencer becomes the fluctuations, and is overcome by the experience. Maharishi refers to this as the object-referral state of consciousness. One is lost in the fear or the anger, the jealousy or the craving, and hence has no sense of being able to stand back from it, understand it, or direct it. With growth of self-referral consciousness, one has a place to stand outside those feelings so that one does not lose control of oneself and one's life.

The experience of *Samadhi* helps any person who is in need of a more balanced emotional life. It is an extremely valuable commodity for both the therapist and the client.

Physiological Approach of *Sattwa Vijaya*

The physiological and pharmacological methods of treating mental and emotional disorders and imbalances in Ayurveda, as described by Charaka, include the following modalities:

1. Purification — *Panchakarma*
2. Herbal and Mineral Compounds — *Dravyaguna*
3. Dietary Measures — *Aharatattva*
4. Daily and Seasonal Routines — *Dinacharya*
5. Exercises for Neuromuscular Integration — *Vyayama*
6. Neurorespiratory Integration — *Pranayama*
7. Five Senses Therapy

1. Purification (*Panchakarma*)

Panchakarma is a set of sophisticated purification procedures designed to eliminate and prevent the accumulation of metabolic impurities within the system. It is said to promote immunity, vitality, and longevity. *Panchakarma* consists of five procedures, including warm oil massage, steam and other heat-generating treatments that serve to loosen up the impurities, and mild laxatives or enemas to flush them out. These procedures come from a very ancient medical tradition, and have only recently been revived in India on a large scale. A hospital in the Indian state of Kerala now uses them expressly for mental illness. There is a growing body of scientific research that demonstrates the mental and physical health benefits of this technology.

2. Herbal and Mineral Compounds (*Dravyaguna*)

Ayurveda has an extensive knowledge of herbs and minerals, including their properties for healing physiological imbalances through proper nourishment of the cells and tissues. I frequently prescribe herbs for a variety of emotional imbalances. For example, one common herb, known as *Brahmi* or a variant of it called *Gotu Kola*, seems to be quite beneficial in alleviating anxiety and insomnia.

Some of the herbal compounds, known as *Rasayanas*

(the Sanskrit term for rejuvenation) have a powerful strengthening effect on the nervous and immune systems. Clinical and laboratory studies have shown them to be helpful in reducing allergy symptoms, retarding and preventing the growth of certain types of cancer cells, reducing some of the symptoms of AIDS, and enhancing immune function. They have also been shown to reduce anxiety and depression.

3. Dietary Measures (*Aharatattva*)

Diet is one of the chief methods mentioned by Charaka for creating or restoring mental and emotional balance. Ayurveda prescribes specific dietary recommendations that take into account the patient's psycho-physiological style (called *Prakriti* in Sanskrit). The *Prakriti* consists of combinations of governing principles of the mind–body, called *Vata*, *Pitta*, and *Kapha*. In addition, the patient's medical condition (*Vikriti*) and the season are taken into account. For example, *Vata* imbalances such as anxiety are best treated with foods that are well cooked and unctuous, and consist of sweet, sour, and salty tastes. Irritability, a *Pitta* imbalance, is best treated with a diet of cooler foods with sweet, bitter, and astringent tastes, and drinks that are room temperature rather than warm. Depression, a *Kapha* imbalance, is best treated with drier foods that are well cooked and have a bitter, astringent, and pungent taste.

Various types of fasting are also prescribed under certain circumstances, especially for *Kapha*-related depression.

4. Daily and Seasonal Routines (*Dinacharya*)

The Charaka Samhita and other Ayurvedic texts suggest patterns of living designed to attune our lifestyle with the natural rhythms of the day and the seasons of the year. For example, the largest meal should be eaten around noon, when the "digestive fire" is said to be highest; light, cooling foods are suggested for the hot summer months, and heavier, warming foods for the dry and cold seasons of fall and winter. These routines (the above being just one example) are modified to suit the constitutional type of each person. Following these recommendations helps to maintain or restore physical and psychological equilibrium.

Ayurveda recommends *Abhyanga*, a daily self-massage with herbalized oil.

The skin is the largest organ of the body, with nerve endings connected throughout the body. A daily massage with herbalized oil has been described in the Ayurvedic texts as having a soothing effect on the mind, nervous system, and endocrine system, as well as increasing flexibility of muscles, tissues, and joints. The procedure is also said to remove impurities on the cellular and tissue levels. The effects of this have been described in Ayurvedic texts as increased softness and luster of the skin, increased energy and clarity of mind, and increased "mental immunity" or equanimity in the face of stressful situations. Research has begun to verify some of these claims.

Administration of medications through the skin is commonly used today in Western medicine. Medicated skin patches are employed to combat air-sickness, to help quit smoking, and to stimulate the heart in cardiac patients. This principle of delivering medicinal substances through the skin was employed thousands of years ago and is frequently prescribed in the three major classical texts of Ayurveda, the Sushruta, Vagbhatta, and Charaka Samhitas.

Another Ayurvedic recommendation is *Nasya*, the placing of a few drops of sesame oil, ghee (clarified butter), or other herbal mixtures, in the nostrils. It's well known in modern medicine that intranasal administration is a very effective way to deliver some medicines, due to the extensive blood supply in the nose. Studies have shown that *Nasya* produces increased clarity of mind and enlivens the senses. It is also an effective treatment for seasonal allergies and sinus conditions. The Ayurvedic texts describe how *Nasya* can help in the prevention and treatment of mental illness.

Maharishi AyurVeda recommends the regular morning and evening practice of the Transcendental Meditation technique, not only for the treatment of a variety of mental disorders, but also for the promotion of ideal mental health and higher states of consciousness. Hundreds of published research studies substantiate these benefits.

Other aspects of daily routine as prescribed by Ayurveda include eating, sleeping, and exercising regularly and at the appropriate time of day.

5. Exercises for Neuromuscular Integration (*Vyayama*)

Vedic exercises for neuromuscular integration (generally known as Yoga postures or *Asanas*) are recommended to improve or restore mind–body coordination. Some exercises are universally recommended (such as the 12-posture cycle known as the "Sun Salutation") while others are suggested according to specific imbalances. These can also be used simply as a preventive measure, to improve the circulation, tone the body, and keep it flexible. In general, these exercises promote balanced physiological functioning. Ayurveda recommends specific Hatha Yoga postures for each of the major psychiatric disorders.

6. Neurorespiratory Integration (*Pranayama*)

Various breathing exercises are prescribed in Ayurveda to restore integrated functioning to all levels of mind and body. In modern science it is becoming increasingly known that by regulating the breathing, one can, for example, lower the blood pressure and heart rate.

In Ayurveda, breathing is understood to be associated with all the natural brain and hormonal rhythms of the body. Regulation of the breathing through recommended breathing exercises can thus stimulate greater health and balance in all these physiological systems. Specific breathing techniques are recommended for specific disorders, as well as for the prevention of mental and emotional imbalance and the promotion of ideal mental health.

Once again, all these physiological approaches are employed in Ayurveda not just for treatment, but are strongly recommended for prevention as well. They are natural, gentle, and non-invasive, produce no negative side effects, and are helpful for maintaining good mental, physical, and emotional health as well as for restoring balance if any disorder arises.

7. Five Senses Therapy

A number of Vedic procedures are used to balance mind and body through the senses. These pleasant and enjoyable therapies include aromatherapy and Gandharva Veda (music therapy). Aromatherapy uses fragrant oils diffused into the air. Modern research is discovering the value of smell in treating psychiatric disorders. For example, researchers at a medical clinic in Chicago have found that the smell of green apples is a good treatment for claustrophobia.

Gandharva Veda is a traditional music therapy to enliven balance throughout the physiology by eliminating the imbalances responsible for emotional as well as physical disorders. An unpublished study at a state mental hospital, for example, showed some very promising clinical benefits to geriatric patients who received daily Gandharva Veda therapy.[6]

There are also therapies in Ayurveda that involve touch (e.g. massage), taste, and color.

Behavioral Approach of *Sattwa Vijaya*

How one behaves in relation to other people is an important element in Maharishi AyurVeda's holistic vision of life. The ancient *Rishis* recognized that certain qualities and ways of treating other people are consistent with natural law and have a positive or life-supporting effect on others and on oneself. These

Sattwa Vijaya: A Balanced Mind Is Victorious

behavioral recommendations are known in the Charaka Samhita as *Sadvritta*, or Behavioral Rasayanas.

The Sanskrit word "*Rasayana*" means rejuvenation. Behavioral Rasayanas refer to those forms of behavior that result in revitalization of the mind, body, and spirit. They are Ayurvedic prescriptions for simultaneously enhancing one's own personal development and making relationships and social interactions more harmonious.

At first glance, the Behavioral Rasayanas may look like just another moralistic list of "do's and don'ts." However, there is a deep rationale behind them. For example, one is urged to speak the sweet truth. The obvious reason for this prescription is because it is better for others if we are kind and diplomatic rather than blunt and harsh. This prescription also benefits ourselves — if we say something that is hurtful to someone else, it is very likely that there will be a negative response in return.

On a deeper level, however, Ayurveda teaches that there is a physiological reality involved in the very doing that immediately affects the doer. According to Ayurveda, our physiology is structured by our experience. The nervous system, mind, and body are designed so that positive thoughts and actions have a harmonious and healing influence on the entire system. If one speaks the pleasant and sweet truth, that act alone has a soothing and beneficial effect upon the physiology. It promotes balance.

On the other hand, if one says something harmful to someone, negative biochemical reactions take place. The role of stress in disease is already well known, and there is a great deal of research showing the role of specific emotions in developing diseases. An example of this relationship is the association between Type A personalities (who tend to drive themselves and others, and manifest more anger and frustration in the process) and heart disease. According to the work that was done by Candace Pert at the National Institute of Mental Health, we have a sophisticated pharmaceutical factory inside our bodies that responds to our thoughts and emotions.[7] For example, if one tells a lie, the resultant feelings of guilt, fear, and shame may have a deleterious effect upon the body.

In other words, every action has a reaction within the physiology itself. If one violates one's own nature by saying or doing things that are unnatural to one's physiology, negative repercussions are unavoidable. Specific biochemical neurotransmitters are related to depression, happiness, anger, contentment, or any mood or thinking pattern. Positive thoughts create "positive molecules" that lead to a healthy physiology; negative thoughts and feelings generate "negative molecules" that are detrimental to health. Ayurveda recommends that even when delivering a mes-

Sattwa Vijaya: A Balanced Mind Is Victorious

sage to someone that might be hard for the person to hear, it can be done in a diplomatic and compassionate way.

Thus, in addition to the social and altruistic benefits of positive behavior, the most immediate benefit is that it engenders an improved state of health for the individual. Since our physiology is created by every choice we make, our behavior becomes a technique that we can use for developing better health and transforming our consciousness. This "technique" is systematized as the Behavioral Rasayanas. Keeping them in mind as a guideline for behavior, and doing our best to follow them, without straining, results in better mental and physical health, as well as more harmonious relationships. A few examples of these guidelines for health are:

- Speak well of others
- Speak the sweet truth
- Respect elders and teachers
- Exercise non-violence
- Perform charity
- Practice forgiveness

Additionally, Maharishi AyurVeda contributes a whole new paradigm to this area of Behavioral Rasayanas because it provides the experience of the field of pure consciousness or Self. This experience is cultured naturally over time through regular practice of the Transcendental Meditation technique. Physicist John Hagelin, PhD, has postulated that the field of pure consciousness is the same field that promotes the balance and harmony that we see in nature. Quantum physics describes this field that underlies and harmonizes all natural functioning, and calls it the unified field. The unified field is to all the laws of nature as a seed is to a tree (and as the DNA is to our physiology). It is the foundation, the organizing element that contains the knowledge that conducts everything we see and know (and don't know) in our universe. By becoming identified with this field, one begins to behave spontaneously in a balanced and harmonious way with oneself and others. So, instead of just learning these behavioral recommendations and trying to follow them as best one can, individuals growing in pure consciousness begin to naturally, and without any contriving or effort, display these very Behavioral Rasayanas in their daily lives.

Treatments that Work on the Level of Mind, Body, and Spirit

Ayurveda also includes an array of therapeutic modalities that operate at a level deeper than the physiological or psychological levels. There are procedures that classical Ayurvedic texts such as the Charaka Samhita refer to as *Daiva Vyapashraya Chikitsa*.

As we learn more about the relationship of Ayurveda and modern science, we can see that this aspect of treatment has to do with what can be referred to as the quantum mechanical level, the link between pure consciousness and the physical body. According to unified field and quantum models of physics, it is at this level that the unified field, through its own self-interacting dynamics, transforms its unified structure and gives rise to the matter and force fields. These fields in turn structure atoms, molecules, and the whole field of material creation. According to unified field and quantum mechanical models in physics, this process of matter manifesting from the field of non-matter is known as "symmetry-breaking" and is known to occur in an orderly, sequential fashion. A number of quantum physicists have postulated, based on their mathematical calculations, that this quantum level includes the entire range of mental and emotional functioning.

This process of matter manifesting from non-matter is going on at all times. It didn't just happen once, at the beginning of creation, but is a dynamic, fluid process that never ceases. If it did stop, the whole universe would simply collapse into nothingness.

Einstein showed the modern world that matter is inter-convertible with energy. Ayurveda knew this truth thousands of years ago, and expressed it in the concept that all matter has wave-like properties. According to Maharishi AyurVeda, the underlying reality is the unified field, which gives rise to pulsating waves of matter and energy that have specific frequencies. This is the quantum level of existence. These frequencies have a sound value, as they have wave functions, and are different for different objects. We don't normally hear those primordial sounds of natural law that are the basis of the formation and functioning of the whole universe, but the ancient Vedic seers are credited with having such settled, subtle awareness that they could actually experience the mechanics of creation within the deep quietness of their own minds.

These seers (*Rishis* in Sanskrit) utilized the principle of resonance to give their discoveries a practical application. Resonance is the phenomenon in which one sound or vibratory frequency evokes the same frequency somewhere else. A common example is when a vibrating tuning fork causes a second tuning fork to spontaneously start vibrating. Vedic seers cognized the reality that certain specific Vedic sounds are correlated with certain parts of our physiology. These cognitions have been passed down to us through the ages by oral tradition.

When a person with a particular kind of imbalance listens to the recitation of these specific sounds, a resonance is created with the particular aspect of the patient's body. In this way, through sound resonance, it is possible to re-balance the mind–body system where imbalance or disorder previously existed. This is the scientific understanding of *Daiva Vyapashraya Chikitsa*. It is a subtle form of treatment, whose theoretical underpinnings are still unknown to modern science. Yet it is considered to be one of the most powerful prescriptions of Ayurveda because it works at the deepest levels of the mind–body system. Examples of *Daiva Vyapashraya Chikitsa* in Ayurveda include the use of a sound (*Mantra*) during meditation. Other treatments using this principle of resonance include Vedic sound therapy (using specific sounds to promote balance in specific organ systems) and music (Gandharva) therapy that uses sound and melody to restore harmony and balance in the individual as well as in the environment.

Daiva Vyapashraya Chikitsa also includes "environmental approaches." These consist of Jyotish, Yagya, and group meditation.

Jyotish and Yagya together form the 5000-year-old system of diagnosis and treatment of physiological and psychological imbalances through a combination of astrology and Vedic recitation (the use of sound to create a prescribed effect) to counteract any negative planetary influences.

Numerous research studies have shown that when the square root of one percent of a population practices the Transcendental Meditation and TM-Sidhi programs together in one place, positive trends increase in the surrounding environment, and negative trends decrease. (The TM-Sidhi program is an advanced program of Transcendental Meditation.)

Human Physiology — Expression of Veda and Vedic Literature

Before concluding this discussion of how Maharishi AyurVeda presents us with a new paradigm for prevention and treatment of mental illness, and for the promotion of higher stages of human consciousness, I would like to mention an important and novel recent discovery that has far-reaching implications for the future of healthcare. This discovery was made by Tony Nader, MD, PhD, and is fully described in his book *Human Physiology, Expression of Veda and the Vedic Literature*.[8]

Through extensive research, and in collaboration with Maharishi Mahesh Yogi, Dr. Nader has discovered that all 40 aspects of the Vedic literature, as delineated by Maharishi, have been found to correspond in structure and function to the human anatomy and physiology. In his book, Dr. Nader shows how this finding ultimately leads to the conclusion that "the Veda is the blueprint of creation — the blueprint which evolves into physical creation." In this book, it becomes crystal clear that the human physiology has its basis in Veda, which in its very structure is eternal and uncreated. When one studies Dr. Nader's discovery in depth, it's possible to see how learning to function at this level of the fundamental impulses of natural law has the potential for transforming how the field of medicine and psychiatry will be practiced in the years to come.

This transformation has already begun to happen through the development of Vedic technologies in which a person can experience Vedic sounds that resonate with particular parts of the brain as well as with components of the entire physiology. The prediction is that when these Vedic vibrations resonate with their corresponding aspects of the physiology, the DNA will re-set in accordance with its original blueprint, resulting in greater health and wholeness. We can foresee a time when these subtle yet powerful forms of treatment will find their way into the mainstream of standard medical practice.

In summary, all of the methodologies that have been discussed in this essay result in *Sattwa Vijaya*, the victorious state of a balanced mind.

Notes

1. Maharishi Mahesh Yogi, *Maharishi Vedic University: Introduction* (The Netherlands: Maharishi Vedic University Press), 260.
2. *Caraka-Samhita Chaukhambha Orientalis, Vols. 1 and 2*, Prof. Priyavrat Sharma (Ed.) (Varanasi & Delhi: Jaikrishnadas Ayurveda Series No. 36).
3. Maharishi Mahesh Yogi, *Maharishi's Absolute Theory of Defence: Sovereignty in Invincibility* (India: Age of Enlightenment Publications, 1996), 554.
4. Maharishi Mahesh Yogi, *Maharishi Mahesh Yogi on the Bhagavad-Gita, A New Translation and Commentary, Chapters 1–6* (Penguin, 1967/1990), 151.
5. Ibid., 98.
6. Brooks and Sorflaten, "The Therapeutic Benefit of Gandharva Veda and Classical Music on Geriatric Psychiatric Patients" (Unpublished, 1987).
7. Candace Pert, *Molecules of Emotion: The Science Behind Mind–Body Medicine* (New York, USA: Touchstone, 1999).
8. T. Nader, *Human Physiology: Expression of Veda and the Vedic Literature* (The Netherlands: Maharishi Vedic University, 1995).

REFLECTIONS ON
MAHARISHI AYURVEDA
AND MENTAL HEALTH

ESSAY 4

The Bhagavad-Gita: A Model for Vedic Counseling

ESSAY 4

The Bhagavad-Gita: A Model for Vedic Counseling

The Bhagavad-Gita is part of the branch of Vedic literature called the Itihasas. The Itihasas can be viewed as historical documents from ancient India, designed to impart practical wisdom that can be applied to the "here and now" of any generation. Bhagavad-Gita is Sanskrit for "The Song of God"; it represents the laws of nature responsible for upholding human life and evolution. The Bhagavad-Gita is part of the epic narrative called the Mahabharata, written down over 5000 years ago by the renowned Vedic sage Vyasa. It can be seen as the quintessential ideal counseling session, a model for therapists to study and emulate for all times to come.[1]

The practical knowledge of how to gain the most from life and how to face any of life's most difficult challenges comes out in the course of a dialogue between two individuals, Lord Krishna and Arjuna. Arjuna is the leading warrior of his time, an archer who finds himself caught in a terrible psycho-emotional dilemma.

A Universal Dilemma

Arjuna is a member of the Pandava family. The Pandavas represent the qualities of righteousness, integrity, goodness, compassion, and nobility. The other family, with whom the Pandavas are at war, the Kauravas, represent the side of deceit, corruption, and evil.

Nonetheless, the Kauravas are Arjuna's blood relatives and friends, and, being a man of unbounded love and compassion, he becomes too paralyzed to take the action of leading his army into battle. On the one hand, his mind knows that the right thing to do is to fight, in order to subdue an evil force that has corrupted his nation. But his highly developed heart is in anguish at the thought of killing his loved ones on the battlefield.

To further complicate his dilemma, Arjuna knows the devastation that can be inflicted by war. His mind is in conflict because of his concern for the disruption of family "*Dharma.*" *Dharma* is the natural force of evolution expressed through traditional family values, family integrity, and one's destined path in life. Arjuna's clear intellect sees how the disruption of war will greatly upset the structural intactness and valued traditions of many families if he chooses to fight. Thus, the first chapter begins by depicting Arjuna, the greatest archer of his time, a man of many achievements and impeccable integrity, in a state of complete confusion and despondency. In fact, at the end of the first chapter, he lays his weapon down and says:

> *Alas! We are resolved to commit*
> *great sin in that we are prepared*
> *to slay our kinsmen ...*
>
> *It were better for me if the sons of*
> *Dhritarashtra, weapons in hand,*
> *should slay me, unresisting and*
> *unarmed in battle.*
>
> (Bhagavad-Gita, I, 45-46)[2]

The chapter ends with the following statement:

> *Having spoken thus at the time of battle,*
> *casting away arrow and bow, Arjuna sat*
> *down on the seat of the chariot, his mind*
> *overwhelmed with sorrow.*
>
> (Bhagavad-Gita, I, 47)

From the point of view of a mental-health professional, this description of Arjuna's conflict is highly relevant to modern day life. The same kind of inner conflict and disharmony between heart and mind is "standard fare" in many of the patients we see. Beyond this, it is not uncommon for even "highly functioning" people today to frequently be faced with the dilemma, "I know this is what I should do, but it just doesn't feel right." How many people in today's society make themselves go to work, but would rather stay home and spend more time with their children?

Even with the more "serious" presentations to a mental-health professional, such as in major depressive disorder, these core conflicts are often at the root of the problem. Such was the case with a recent patient of mine, "Martha," who was immobilized by depression as a result of having left her husband of 15 years because their marriage was "boring" and in her words, "we have nothing in common." After leaving her husband, she was beginning to regret her decision, because she felt it was "bad for the children." She was unable to function at work, take care of her four children, or do her housework as a result of being overwhelmed by her dilemma.

So, Arjuna's conflict is in essence archetypal. It represents one of the most common causes of human suffering. Even though Arjuna was a "high functioning" person, with a highly developed heart and mind, he still was feeling caught in the web of the inner workings of his own mind. The symptoms he suffered from — anxiety, depression, mental confusion, immobility — are among the most common symptoms seen by mental-health professionals today. In essence, Arjuna's predicament is a metaphor applicable to all generations, including our own. The fact that Arjuna is such a brave, noble, compassionate, and respectable individual is apropos, since it points out that we are all susceptible to life's vicissitudes, and at times we all can benefit from some outside counseling or advice.

An Enlightened Guide

Arjuna has Lord Krishna as his guide and mentor — his therapist, if you will — to help him out of his miserable state. Krishna represents the quintessence of the ideal teacher, or *Guru* — he is at peace with himself, deeply contented in his own personal life, and therefore able to be completely compassionate and yet remain objective. Honored in the Vedic literature as an embodiment of total natural law — of divinity — Krishna is said to be a storehouse of Vedic wisdom, and is thus an example of fully integrated and enlightened life, full of love and devotion toward the betterment of his fellow man.

He also represents the qualities of an ideal therapist. His timing is impeccable — he knows just when to speak the appropriate words that help move Arjuna along in his quest for knowledge. Arjuna needs to gain a broader perspective of his situation, so that he can make the correct decisions about what is best for the evolution of both himself and his environment.

At different times, Krishna is stern, respectful, loving, educational, supportive, scolding, silent — whatever Arjuna needs at any given moment. He is so skillful that the entire discourse of the "Vedic counseling session" lasted only two hours. This was enough to take Arjuna from the depths of depression, hopelessness, and despair, to the highest level of human development — enlightenment.

I would like to share with you an example of Krishna's use of tact and timing to facilitate Arjuna's evolution during this Vedic counseling session. In the following example, Arjuna is overwhelmed with anger, and ready to plunge into battle. This is a metaphor that denotes how often anger leads to impulsive action, which almost always ends up making the situation worse. In the field of mental health, the presenting symptom is often anger associated with some impulsive act — it could be anything from aggressiveness directed towards oneself or others, to quitting one's job or leaving one's relationship.

In many instances, such as with Arjuna, individuals may be on the verge of taking some action that they might later regret, but they come in asking for advice on how to get hold of their emotions and gain a broader perspective on their situation. They desire to gain some equanimity, some balance of mind, so that they'll be able to make a decision that is intelligent, appropriate, and life-supporting for themselves and others.

In Chapter 1 of the Bhagavad-Gita, Krishna — who is acting as Arjuna's charioteer — recognizes Arjuna's dilemma and immediately starts the therapeutic process:

> … *thus invoked by Gudakesha (Arjuna),*
> *Hrishikesha (Lord Krishna), having drawn*
> *up the magnificent chariot*
> *between the two armies,*
>
> *Before Bhishma and Drona and all*
> *the rulers of the earth, said: Partha (Arjuna)!*
> *behold these Kurus gathered together.*
> (Bhagavad-Gita, I, 24-25)

Maharishi Mahesh Yogi's commentary eloquently describes Krishna's therapeutic skill in his quest to assist Arjuna in his time of crisis:

> Lord Krishna had seen that Arjuna was outraged. Anger is a great enemy; it reduces one's strength. And his charioteer does not like to see Arjuna's strength waning. Lord Krishna is required to do something to restore Arjuna to his normal stature. But this alone will not suffice; something more is necessary to make

Arjuna really strong. Anger in him indicates that he is not really strong, for anger is a sign of weakness. Lord Krishna knows that Arjuna, although the greatest archer of his time, has not been given the real secret of warfare. He has been taught the art of archery, but he has not been trained to shoot his arrows while remaining firm in himself. If an archer shoots while he is angry, his anger will make him weak.

Arjuna has called Lord Krishna "Achyuta," which means firm and unmoved. This is what Lord Krishna has to teach Arjuna to be. But wisdom cannot be given to a man unless he asks for it and shows his readiness to receive it. It is therefore necessary for Lord Krishna to arouse in Arjuna the need and desire to learn. It would have been demoralizing if Arjuna had been told on the battlefield that he needed to know the art of being firm. He had to recognize this for himself; only then could Lord Krishna help him. To produce the desired result in Arjuna, the Lord speaks one short sentence:

"Partha! behold these Kurus gathered together." This is the first utterance of Lord Krishna in the Bhagavad-Gita, the first word of advice to Arjuna on the battlefield.

The miracle it produced in Arjuna has for centuries escaped the attention of practically every commentator, and in consequence, Arjuna is portrayed as a confused mental wreck. A close study of the commentary on the following verses will reveal the true nature of Arjuna's condition.

Lord Krishna addresses Arjuna as "Partha," the son of Pritha. With this expression, He reminds Arjuna of his mother and thereby creates a warm wave of love in his heart, the warmth of love that connects son and mother. It is this tender bond of love that develops into all family and social relationships, that maintains a family, a society, a nation and a world.

Having created this wave of love in Arjuna's heart, Lord Krishna desires to strengthen it; and for this He says: "behold these Kurus gathered together." This quickens all the ways of the heart, where different relationships are held in different shades of love. Seeing all his dear ones "together" in one glance, his whole heart swells with love.

It is a marvel to observe Krishna's skill in facilitating the process of Arjuna's "treatment," the goal of which is nothing short of promoting higher states of consciousness. What is even more marvelous, in my opinion, is the subsequent knowledge that Krishna unfolds to Arjuna — the knowledge of how to resolve his dilemma and rise out of the field of suffering altogether.

Knowledge of the Solution

Krishna teaches Arjuna how to perform action, which in Arjuna's case is to lead his army into battle. But, as Krishna points out, what is important is not only what we do, but how we experience it. It is the inner process of living from moment to moment that is all-important. We all have our given *Dharma*, or chosen profession, whether it be custodial work, medicine, law, teaching, or home-making. The important question is, according to the Bhagavad-Gita, "What is the quality of our experience throughout the day?"

Here is the essence of Vedic wisdom, brought to light so clearly in the context of this Vedic counseling session. In a very well organized and systematic way, Krishna reveals to Arjuna that what is important in order to enjoy life to the fullest is balance — balance of mind, emotions, and behavior. A balanced mind is a clear mind, which is capable of clear perception and understanding of any given situation. It is a mind free from conflict. Mental conflict is due to lack of creativity, lack of the ability to see the situation clearly enough to find the answer to any particular problem that arises.

On the emotional level, balance refers to the experience of inner peace and contentment — feeling

The Bhagavad-Gita: A Model for Vedic Counseling

confident, unshaken, and secure in the face of life's challenges. Balanced behavior refers to action that is in accord with natural law, that is, action that effortlessly promotes happiness and well-being in oneself and others.

> *That yogi is said to be united who is contented in knowledge and experience, unshakeable, master of the senses, who is balanced in experiencing earth, stone or gold.*
>
> (Bhagavad-Gita, VI, 8)

Maharishi's commentary on this verse states that "he is a yogi whose life is marked by a balanced state of mind throughout all experience in the field of diversity" and that "Although they may differ in mode of life and manner of activity, those who are realized have this in common: they always possess balanced understanding and vision."

The Bhagavad-Gita provides practical knowledge that in my opinion is highly applicable to the field of mental health. Krishna conveys to Arjuna the sequence of psychic events that result in mental conflict and emotional pain. He then explains how balance of mind and emotions can be accomplished, resulting in a direct reversal of the process that led to the mental and emotional suffering.

Lord Krishna describes the cause of imbalance as follows:

> *Pondering on objects of the senses,*
> *a man develops attachment for them;*
> *from attachment springs up desire,*
> *and desire gives rise to anger.*
>
> *From anger arises delusion; from delusion*
> *unsteadiness of memory; from unsteadiness*
> *of memory destruction of intellect; through*
> *the destruction of the intellect he perishes.*
>
> (Bhagavad-Gita, II, 62-63)

Maharishi's commentary on these two verses elucidates these mechanics of the formation of many psychological disturbances commonly seen in everyday practice:

> Anger excites the mind, which loses its balance and power of discrimination; it loses proper vision and foresight and a right sense of values. This state of "delusion" obscures the track of memory, and thereby one feels as if disconnected from the harmonious rhythm of life. Wisdom fails, and the intellect ceases to function. The boat of life is left with nobody in control; it meets with disaster as a matter of course.

These mechanics can be applied to problems ranging from addictions (drugs, alcohol, eating, sex, gambling, etc.) to depression and anxiety. For example, addiction, regardless of type, is based on a strong attachment to the object of sensory pleasure. Take the case of "Maria," a young professional woman with an eating addiction. She typically binged at night, when she felt a sense of lack, experienced as "anxious emptiness." Once she started binging, she got temporary relief, but later felt angry with herself, which in turn resulted in her being "deluded" into thinking she was a worthless individual with no ability to control herself. The resulting low self-esteem and depression ended up interfering with her ability to function, both in her personal and her professional life.

I have found these dynamics of mental illness to be present as a causative factor in a great majority of individuals with whom I work. The value of this age-old knowledge is that one can see the chain of events of imbalance and can therefore stop the whole process by dealing with the first step of transformation toward imbalance. The first step is the attachment of the senses to the object of experience, whether it is food, a drug, some material possession, or another person. Of course, the reason for the attachment in the first place is some feeling of lack of inner peace and contentment, requiring one to seek inner satisfaction from the outside.

Reflections on *Maharishi AyurVeda* and Mental Health

Transcending to Relieve Suffering

Here lies the key to treatment of any mental suffering, according to the Bhagavad-Gita. Krishna assures Arjuna that his worries will evaporate once he steps out of the field of desire and thinking, and therefore out of attachment altogether. He advises Arjuna that as long as his sense of self and well-being are dependent upon outside events, he can never completely escape from experiencing conflict, confusion, anxiety, and unhappiness. According to the Bhagavad-Gita, pleasure gained from outside sources alone often results in frustration and disappointment. This is because either (a) one is unable to attain it in the first place, or (b) if one attains what one wants, it ultimately doesn't last.

> *All pleasures born of contact are only sources*
> *of sorrow; they have a beginning and an end,*
> *O son of Kunti. The enlightened man does not*
> *rejoice in them.*
> (Bhagavad-Gita, V, 22)

So, if an individual can resolve the issue of object-referral, that is, over-attachment to objects, as the intended source of happiness in life, he or she holds the key to preventing mental conflict and emotional pain. The key to releasing attachment, restoring mental balance, and creating inner peace and tranquility is shown to Arjuna by Krishna. This is explained, with commentary by Maharishi, as follows:

> *Therefore he whose senses are all withdrawn from their objects, O mighty-armed, his intellect is established.*
>
> (Bhagavad-Gita, II, 68)

Maharishi comments on this verse that:

It gives the quintessence of the entire scheme of fulfilment in life, which is to channel the mind into regions of experience more blissful than the ordinary gross fields of sensory life.

"Therefore" refers back to the words of verse 66: "for one without peace how can there be happiness?" It indicates that if happiness is sought, peace has to be created, the nervous system has to be brought to a state of restful alertness. For this to happen, the activity of the senses must cease. That is why the Lord says: "whose senses are all withdrawn from their objects."

The verse establishes that the senses lose their relationship to their objects when the intellect is resolute, when it is established in the Self.

The senses function on different levels. On the gross level they enable the mind to enjoy the external aspects of their objects. Functioning on subtler levels, they enable it to experience the more subtle aspects of objects; and joys arising from the experience of the subtler states of objects are greater than those arising from their gross states.

When, during meditation, the mind begins to experience the subtler aspects of a thought, it experiences increasing charm and thus is naturally attracted to the experience of the subtlest aspect of the thought. The experience of this finest state of thought, which is on the subtlest level of creation, provides the mind with the greatest joy in the field of relativity, but even this joy is not permanent, is not of absolute nature.

Arjuna is being directed to bring his mind to a state beyond the greatest joy of relativity, so that he can free himself from dependence upon the transitory relative joys of life and become established in the bliss of the Absolute. To reach this eternal bliss, the Lord asks him to leave completely the field of sensory perception, both gross and subtle. Thus he will come to established intellect, intellect established in the Transcendent. To live this principle in daily life is simple, for one need only know how to allow the mind to come quite naturally out of the field of the senses and reach the state of established intellect.

Maharishi, in his commentary, explains that the regular practice of meditation is pivotal if one is to achieve this state of "non-attachment." Forcibly abstaining from the objects of sensory experience will only create strain. Non-attachment that results from the experience of one's inner Self through the regular process of transcending, is a natural state. It is based in the mind being satisfied where it is, and therefore not needing to seek satisfaction elsewhere.

What results from regular experience of transcendence is the integration of Transcendental Consciousness — as Maharishi calls the state of restful alertness — with thought and activity. This integration, when fully developed, is identified by Maharishi as Cosmic Consciousness. When the mind is stationed in restful alertness, whether one is awake, dreaming, or sleeping, one has the spontaneous experience of "witnessing." This is the experience of the inner Self being naturally unattached to the field of thought, emotions, and outer activity. This state of human development, resulting from the regular practice of Transcendental Meditation, allows a person to be impermeable to stress. In the following verse of the Bhagavad-Gita, "him" refers to this inner Self.

> *Weapons cannot cleave him, nor fire*
> *burn him; water cannot wet him, nor*
> *wind dry him away.*
> (Bhagavad-Gita, II, 23)

Not only does such an enlightened individual experience freedom from stress, but also freedom from all suffering, being fully content inside himself or herself. A description of this natural state of non-attachment, born of contact with the Self, follows:

> *Having cast off all attachment to the*
> *fruit of action, ever contented, depending*
> *on nothing, even though fully engaged in*
> *action he does not act at all.*
> (Bhagavad-Gita, IV, 20)

The value of a technique for regular transcending is apparent. What is even more inspiring, as Lord Krishna boldly explains, is that this teaching is universally applicable to anyone.

> *Even if you were the most sinful of all*
> *sinners, you would cross over all evil by*
> *the raft of knowledge alone.*
> (Bhagavad-Gita, IV, 36)

Maharishi's commentary on this verse says:

Enlightenment is irrespective of anything in the relative field; nothing can be an obstacle to enlightenment. However dense the darkness and however long it may have existed, one ray of the rising sun is enough to dispel the darkness, though it takes time to reach the brightness of the mid-day sun. Even a momentary flash of transcendental consciousness is enough to dispel the delusion of ignorance, though it takes time to gain full enlightenment.

Maharishi refers to enlightenment as a state in which "one has crossed over all evil by the raft of knowledge" and comments that "This brings hope even to a man whose life may be full of wrongdoing." He adds: "This verse recommends taking refuge in knowledge [of the Self] in order to rise above the possibility of any sin in life and promises redemption even to the worst sinner in the world." This terminology of sin can be understood in our modern world as stress, illness, or physiological impurity and is not meant to have any religious connotation.

Maharishi, in his commentaries on Chapter II, verse 40, and throughout Chapter VI, describes the mechanics of the ideal way to practice meditation. The key ingredients are that it should be:

- **Effortless**

    "In this Yoga, no effort is lost and no obstacle exists." (II, 40)

- **Natural**

The technique utilizes the nature of the mind, which is to seek increasing charm. The mind, with no effort whatsoever, moves in the direction of greater charm, which naturally exists at the finer, more subtle levels of the thought process.

Additional characteristics of the ideal form of meditation, due to its inherent naturalness, include that it is reliable, time-tested, and universally applicable.

Maharishi describes the technique he revived from the Vedic tradition — following a long period when it had been lost to the world — as having all these characteristics, and being the quickest and most direct route to develop higher states of consciousness. He named the technique he founded the Transcendental Meditation technique. This actually describes the process: a mental technique (meditation) in which the meditator transcends (goes beyond) the active levels of the mind and reaches the field of silence, pure consciousness or inner wakefulness.

Any counseling that incorporates Vedic principles should involve a person learning to transcend regularly. This cultivates the mind to dwell in the transcendental field while it continues to be engaged in the various modes of day-to-day life. Not losing the experience of one's inner Self allows one to more fully enjoy any experience in life, whether it be playing tennis, driving a car, working, or playing with one's children.

One might ask, "If a person is remaining unattached to the experience, how can he or she enjoy it more than if he or she is strongly attached to it?" The answer to this seeming paradox has to do with balance. Without being fully established in the experience of one's Self, life is out of balance. When pure consciousness, characterized by the experience of inner freedom and bliss, is not fully stabilized, then one is naturally "over-identified" with the objects of experience. Becoming a slave to the object, one does not feel free, and therefore one loses the ability to fully appreciate it.

If being "unattached" sounds boring, don't worry, it's not. According to the Vedic system of knowledge, being in higher states of consciousness is supremely enjoyable and blissful at every moment. In the state of enlightenment one enjoys the process of living fully in the here and now. It is only a stressed mind, one that has not experienced the inner peace that comes from transcending regularly, that has the tendency to worry about the past and the future, losing the opportunity to fully appreciate the moment! In Maharishi's commentary to Chapter V, verses 8–9, of the Bhagavad-Gita he states (using the term "Being" to refer to one's inner Self):

> When, through the practice of Transcendental Meditation, cosmic consciousness has been gained, and the individual ego has expanded to cosmic status, the mind automatically functions from the level of its full potentiality and the senses, having reached

their maximum development, function at their highest capacity. The objects of sense, however, remain in their unchanged state. That is why the senses, acting from their raised level, experience objects more completely, resulting in an even greater appreciation of the objects and thus providing experience of greater happiness on the sensory level. This creates a situation in which the objects of sense are enjoyed more thoroughly than before, but because Being is more fully grounded in the very nature of the mind, the impressions of sensory experience fail to capture the mind. The enlightened man thus naturally remains in a state where the senses continue to experience their objects while he remains free.

Applying Vedic Principles to Counseling

There are many forms of counseling and therapy available today, designed to help people cope with a whole range of problems and life issues. There are many schools of therapy, such as insight-oriented, cognitive-behavioral, and supportive. Psychiatrists often combine one of these forms of therapy with medication, such as antidepressants or antipsychotics.

If one studies the interaction in which Lord Krishna uplifts Arjuna to the state of enlightenment, it is possible to develop a model for incorporating Vedic principles

The Bhagavad-Gita: A Model for Vedic Counseling

into counseling that extends far beyond the conventional counseling model. Certainly, conventional therapy has an important role to play in helping individuals gain a better perspective on their problems, as well as attempting to resolve them, by talking about them. The Vedic approach to counseling shares these goals as well, but its purpose extends even further.

The goal of counseling, from the Vedic point of view, is not only to help a person resolve his or her conflicts, but to learn skills for cultivating the mind and nervous system in the direction of higher states of consciousness. In other words, the person coming in for Vedic-oriented counseling could have mild or even more serious psychological problems, but this type of counseling could also benefit any "healthy and normal" person who is seeking to gain the fruits of Vedic wisdom — enlightenment.

The counseling seen in the Bhagavad-Gita presents a completely new paradigm in the field of mental health. The first, and most important, feature that differentiates Vedic counseling from "conventional" counseling is that the "seeker" is taught a meditation technique that allows him or her to regularly and effortlessly transcend. This technique of transcending, epitomized by Transcendental Meditation, when practiced twice daily, results in steady growth toward higher states of consciousness. The direct experience of one's higher Self quickly lifts the seeker out of the field of duality and conflict.

My experience with patients who learn the Transcendental Meditation technique is that almost immediately they experience great relief from their symptoms. This is what Lord Krishna means when he says:

> *Even a little of this dharma*
> *delivers from great fear.*
>
> (Bhagavad-Gita, II, 40)

My patients frequently compare the start of their meditation practice to "turning on a light in a dark room."

For many people, the experience of regularly transcending is in itself curative. Beyond alleviating the individual's symptoms or problems, the technique allows a person to become self-sufficient in his or her own mental healthcare. He or she can continue to grow and mature even after the counseling sessions are over.

In addition to meditation, there are other unique components to the Vedic counseling experience.

Knowledge (*Gyan* and *Vigyan*)

Knowledge has two aspects, intellectual understanding and direct personal experience (*Gyan* and *Vigyan*). As Lord Krishna states:

Truly there is in this world nothing so purifying as knowledge; he who is perfected in Yoga, of himself in time finds this within himself.
(Bhagavad-Gita, IV, 38)

Maharishi explains:

The real nature of life is absolute bliss-consciousness; this crystal water of life has been polluted by becoming mixed with the activities of the three gunas [see p. 150]. This has resulted in masking the eternity of life behind its transient and ever-changing aspects.

The pure state of Being is realized by knowing the relative and the absolute components of life. This knowing comes to perfection when the knower gains perfect intimacy with Being and becomes fully aware of the basic activity of life, the activity of the three gunas as separate from Being. Perfect intimacy with Being is gained when the mind gains the transcendental state of consciousness. This is the absolute state of knowledge, which can be described as the state of knowingness. When knowledge becomes perfect, it arrives at the state of knowingness and brings life to perfect purity. In this way knowledge removes ignorance, which is the greatest impurity of life, and takes life out of the cycle of birth, death and suffering.

The experience of the "knowingness" of one's own true nature, pure consciousness, is the most important knowledge to gain from counseling, according to Maharishi. But there is a definite role for intellectual understanding as well.

> *He who has renounced action by virtue of Yoga, O winner of wealth, whose doubts are rent asunder by knowledge, who is possessed of the Self, him actions do not bind.*
> (Bhagavad-Gita, IV, 41)

Maharishi, in his commentary, explains:

Having stated that renunciation is achieved through the practice of Karma Yoga [the Yoga of action], the Lord here clarifies a very practical point on the path of enlightenment. As the practice of Karma Yoga advances, one begins to feel one's Self as separate from activity. This experience brings with it a feeling of confusion. One finds oneself active and yet inwardly one feels somewhat aloof from activity. Doubts begin to arise in the mind, and the intellect seeks for some explanation of the situation. Right understanding about the ultimate Reality is provided by the teaching of the preceding forty verses; when a man attains cosmic consciousness, the knowledge that Being is independent and separate from activity confirms that his experience is valid. It is this knowledge that removes all doubt about the nature of Reality. Without proper understanding, even the direct experience of eternal freedom may be found to create confusion and fear. The glory of knowledge is extolled here.

The goal of Vedic-style counseling is not only to relieve symptoms, but to guide the seeker in the development of his or her full potential. It emphasizes both direct experience and the intellectual understanding necessary to clarify one's experiences on the path of growth. It also helps inspire the seeker to stay regular in his or her experiential practice of meditation and the other techniques of Maharishi AyurVeda. If a person finds a stone but does not have knowledge of its real value as a diamond, he is liable to cast it off without thinking much about it. If its real worth is known, however, he will treasure it forever.

Therefore, Vedic-oriented counseling contains a strong psycho-educational and cognitive behavioral component. Important elements are detailed below.

1. Knowledge of Higher States of Consciousness

The Bhagavad-Gita is replete with descriptions of how, through the regular alternation between Transcendental Consciousness and daily activity, the higher states of consciousness delineated by Maharishi — Cosmic Consciousness, God Consciousness, and Unity Consciousness — spontaneously develop. Clinical experience in working with Transcendental Meditation practitioners has shown that understanding this process is tremendously valuable to stabilize and support the meditator's evolving experience. Maharishi has developed a 33-lesson videotape course called *The Science of Creative Intelligence* that includes a clear description of this process, and my recommendation is that elements of this course might be included in the counseling sessions.

2. Knowledge of the Process of Purification

When a snowplow moves forward, two things occur. The vehicle moves forward, but also the obstacles on the road are removed. When a person is on the path to higher states of consciousness, most of the time he or she experiences the fruits of transcending, such as more clarity of thinking, more energy, more bliss. But at times the process of physiological purification, which is the actual process of clearing the obstacles, dominates one's experience.

This process, which is essentially the release of deep-rooted stresses from the system, must be clearly understood by the seeker, so that he or she may be patient with any temporary discomfort that may come up from time to time. Vedic counseling includes specific techniques one can practice at these times to facilitate the process of purification in an easy and comfortable manner.

3. Codes of Conduct

The Bhagavad-Gita contains very definite behavioral recommendations to facilitate the growth of consciousness. Some examples follow:

> *Humility (absence of pride), integrity (absence of deceit), non-violence, patience, uprightness, service to the teacher, purity (of body and mind), steadfastness and self-control*
>
> *Constancy in the knowledge of the Spirit, insight into the end of the knowledge of truth — this is declared to be true knowledge and all that is different from it is non-knowledge.*
>
> (Bhagavad-Gita, XIII, 7, 9, 11 — translated by Radhakrishnan)[3]

Even though regular practice of the Transcendental Meditation technique spontaneously results in more healthy and harmonious behavior, it is often quite useful to study and even memorize these codes of conduct. As a result, these effortless intentions on the subtle level of one's awareness help to support our behavior to be more in accordance with natural law. As the mind becomes more powerful from the regular practice of meditation, intentions floating in the subtle levels of awareness easily come to fruition. If a counselor is aware of these behavioral guidelines, he or she can prescribe them to the seeker at opportune times.

4. Knowledge of Personality Types

In the Bhagavad-Gita, three basic constituents of nature — which are also reflected in personality types — are discussed. Most people have a mixture of various proportions of the three in their make-up. These personality types include mental, emotional, and behavioral characteristics. The three constituents are known as *Sattwa*, *Rajas*, and *Tamas*. (The following quote is from a book using an alternative transliteration of *Sattwa*.)

> *The three modes (gunas), goodness (sattva), passion (rajas) and dullness (tamas) born of nature (prakriti), bind down in the body, O mighty-armed Arjuna, the imperishable dweller in the body.*
>
> *Of these, goodness (sattva), being pure, causes illumination and health. It binds, O blameless one, by attachment to happiness and by attachment to knowledge.*

> *Passion (rajas), know thou, is of the nature of attraction, springing from craving and attachment. It binds fast, O son of Kunti (Arjuna), the embodied one by attachment to action.*
>
> *But dullness (tamas), know thou, is born of ignorance and deludes all embodied beings. It binds, O Bharata (Arjuna), by developing the qualities of negligence, indolence, and sleep.*
>
> *Greed, activity, the undertaking of actions, unrest and craving — these spring up, O best of the Bharatas (Arjuna) when rajas increases.*
>
> *Unillumination, inactivity, negligence, and mere delusion — these arise, O joy of the Kurus (Arjuna), when tamas increases.*
>
> *When the light of knowledge streams forth in all the gates of the body, then it may be known that goodness (sattva) has increased.*
>
> (Bhagavad-Gita, selected verses from Chapter XIV — translated by Radhakrishnan)

The beauty of the teaching about personality types in the Bhagavad-Gita is that anyone, no matter where he or she starts, can "turn-up" the level of *Sattwa* and hence change the balance among the three *Gunas*. The regular practice of Maharishi AyurVeda techniques (see below) causes this to happen in a natural and spontaneous fashion. This is a truly inspiring aspect of the counseling, exemplified in the Bhagavad-Gita, which is thousands of years old, since modern psychology has held for years that personality change is very difficult to accomplish.

Maharishi AyurVeda Therapies

In addition to the Transcendental Meditation technique, the Bhagavad-Gita contains an abundance of not only theoretical, but also practical knowledge from Ayurveda (natural healthcare). The Bhagavad-Gita brings out the most salient principles of Ayurveda. One of the most important of these principles is *moderation in all behavior.*

> *Yoga, indeed, is not for him who eats too much nor for him who does not eat at all, O Arjuna; it is not for him who is too much given to sleep nor yet for him who keeps awake.*
>
> *For him who is moderate in food and recreation, moderate of effort in actions, moderate in sleep and waking, for him is the Yoga which destroys sorrow.*
>
> (Bhagavad-Gita, VI, 16–17)

The Bhagavad-Gita: A Model for Vedic Counseling

In Maharishi's commentary on these verses, he states:

The present verse explains the general mode of conduct which alone will allow the bliss experienced in meditation to be infused into the relative phase of existence. Its entire purpose is to warn the aspirant against laying too much importance on any one aspect of relative life. If only he takes things in their due proportion, every aspect of his life will remain without strain. It is this harmonious level of existence which provides the basis on which the divine Being can be lived in the world.

As a part of Vedic-oriented counseling, the seeker should gain in-depth knowledge of how to properly structure his or her daily routine to promote optimal mental and physical health. In addition, the following approaches of Maharishi AyurVeda might be employed.

1. Music Therapy

The music therapy of Maharishi AyurVeda (called Gandharva Veda) could be a part of the patient's daily homework, and could also be utilized during the counseling sessions, in order to generate bliss and promote more creative thinking. During counseling, the mind should be peaceful and still, not agitated, so that it can be most creative in finding solutions to the problems one is wanting to resolve.

2. Yoga and Breathing Exercises

These neuromuscular and neurorespiratory integration techniques are very helpful in promoting and stabilizing the growth of higher states of consciousness. Since infusing the nervous system with the experience of transcendental pure consciousness is the most powerful "vaccine" against mental imbalance, these exercises should be a welcome addition to the counseling program.

3. Knowledge of One's Psycho-physiological Style (*Prakriti*)

As mentioned in the previous essay, the role that *Vata*, *Pitta*, and *Kapha* play in the formation of one's psycho-physiological functioning can help the patient structure his or her diet and daily and seasonal routines for maximum health and balance. If one learns how to promote a healthy mind and body through proper diet, exercise, daily oil massage, and so on, growth of consciousness is greatly facilitated. This is because the nervous system is the reflector of universal consciousness — if we properly take care of and nurture our physical structure, we greatly enhance our spiritual progress.

4. Herbal Therapies

Both clinical experience and emerging scientific research indicate that the use of specific, time-tested, natural herbal preparations can be helpful not only for symptom relief, but also to enhance immunity and develop higher states of consciousness.

Guiding Principles

In summary, it is evident that counseling modeled from this ancient treatise offers much more than "symptom relief." It provides a wonderful opportunity for anyone to learn how to directly experience the inner transcendental nature of his or her being. Furthermore, the patient will develop practical strategies for enhancing the development of his or her full human potential. It employs a mix of insight-oriented (psycho-dynamic), supportive, cognitive-behavioral, psycho-educational, and biological approaches.

To conclude, I would like to summarize a few of the guiding principles of the counseling process found in the Bhagavad-Gita, and hypothesize how they might be adapted to our modern framework of psychotherapy.

In general, the counseling period could be of relatively brief duration, perhaps five to fifteen sessions in most cases. After all, it took Lord Krishna only two hours to fully enlighten Arjuna! This will not only promote self-sufficiency, but will be a significant cost-savings to insurance companies as well as to the person undergoing counseling.

The process of Vedic counseling as a whole should not be a stressful experience. The process should be easy, smooth, comfortable, and blissful at every stage. Sometimes, in the process of transformation from one stage of development to another, an individual may experience some restlessness or discomfort. In such instances, the individual should be shown techniques that will allow him or her to move through these transitions easily and comfortably.

Psychotherapists who have been trained in Maharishi AyurVeda are finding it very helpful to study the Bhagavad-Gita in detail in order to explore the "play-by-play" dynamics of the interaction between Lord Krishna and Arjuna. This enables them to apply the Vedic principles of counseling to their sessions with their clients.

For example, Lord Krishna at first listened patiently to Arjuna, to help him vent his frustrations and clarify the causes of his predicament and the reasons for his seeking help in resolving it. This, along with Krishna's compassion and kindness, helped Arjuna develop the needed trust and receptivity — both necessary ingredients for counseling to be successful. Further along, the experiential techniques and intellectual understanding are brought out tactfully and with exquisite timing.

The Bhagavad-Gita is an ancient record of a masterfully executed Vedic counseling session. The dialogue between Lord Krishna and Arjuna serves as a model for mental-health professionals who are interested not only in helping their clients alleviate suffering, but also in helping them realize the furthest reaches of their human potential.

Notes

1. See also an article by Michael C. Dillbeck, "The Bhagavad-Gita: A Case Study in Vedic Psychology," *Modern Science and Vedic Science* 4:2 (1991).

2. All quotes, and associated commentary, from chapters one to six of the Bhagavad-Gita are from *Maharishi Mahesh Yogi on the Bhagavad-Gita, A New Translation and Commentary, Chapters 1–6* (Penguin Books, 1967/1990).

3. Quotes from chapters seven to eighteen of the Bhagavad-Gita are from S. Radhakrishnan, *The Bhagavadgita* (India: Blackie & Son, 1970).

Conclusion

This book was written with the intention of helping to bring about a paradigm shift in the way health professionals and the public in general view mental health.

Mental illness is viewed as something that is a fait accompli. That is, there is not much you can do to prevent it, and once you have it you are stuck with it. Though medications can help to reduce symptoms, and therapy can help people cope better with their illnesses, up until now there hasn't been a good strategy for primary prevention of mental illness, nor have there been effective natural strategies, without side effects, for its treatment. Especially, there has been no technology in the mental-health field for affording those who are considered normal, healthy people the opportunity to grow to higher states of consciousness — which essentially means that an individual has a 24-hour-a-day experience of very high levels of expanded awareness, intelligence, creativity, inner peace, and contentment.

There have been well over 600 published studies demonstrating that the therapeutic technologies of Maharishi

AyurVeda benefit mental and physical health. There are many studies showing how Maharishi AyurVeda can directly reduce symptoms and help people better cope with anxiety, depression, schizophrenia, sleep disorders, ADHD, and substance-abuse disorders, as well as a whole host of psychosomatic disorders such as asthma, hypertension, heart disease, gastrointestinal disorders, and other chronic diseases. During the course of my 35-plus years of being a mental-health practitioner, I have recommended Maharishi AyurVeda treatments to hundreds of patients. I have had the opportunity to witness my patients gain significant symptom improvement in many of these psychiatric and medical conditions, which has been very gratifying.

What I love about Maharishi AyurVeda is that it has the potential to serve as a "mental-illness vaccine" for the population at large. In particular, the Transcendental Meditation technique, one of the key treatment modalities of Maharishi AyurVeda, when practiced on a regular basis, affords a person the opportunity to experience a level of deep rest evidenced by repeated physiological measures. This regular, profound rest removes deep levels of stress and fatigue, and strongly enhances self-repair mechanisms including at the level of the DNA, and at the cellular, tissue, organ, mind, and emo-

Conclusion

tional levels. This regular deep and refreshing rest promotes the experience, based on greater physiological balance, of increased mental clarity, more calmness and inner peace, and higher levels of joy and contentment.

The effects of this mental-illness vaccine are already evident based on epidemiological research studies. Statistics from companies with measurable numbers of Transcendental Meditation practitioners reveal that, in almost every disease category, utilization of both inpatient and outpatient services is significantly less in the Transcendental Meditation practitioners as compared to the non-meditating group. This has profound implications for cost savings, and the potential of cutting healthcare costs.

In addition, numerous sociological studies have demonstrated that when large groups of individuals come together to practice the advanced TM-Sidhi program in areas of high crime or war, statistically significant reductions in crime rate, suicide rate, and war deaths are seen. On the positive side, improvement in societal measures such as the stock market, employment rates, and reporting of positive-news events are also seen where these large groups of advanced meditators convene.

In this book I have explained how Maharishi Ayur-Veda, although coming from an ancient tradition, has tremendous implications for being helpful in our modern world. Its potential is not only for primary and secondary mental-health prevention, but also for treatment: its modalities have been shown to be helpful in treatment of a variety of mental disorders.

The implications for enhanced societal and global mental health are truly exciting.

About the Author

Jim Brooks, MD, has spent his life helping people create health for themselves through natural medicine. He is a practicing psychiatrist who has studied and practiced Maharishi AyurVeda for many years. He received extensive training in Ayurveda from some of the most renowned *Vaidyas* (Ayurvedic physicians) in India. Dr. Brooks was the founding medical director of the Maharishi AyurVeda Health Centers in Los Angeles and Washington, DC. He is also a teacher of the Transcendental Meditation technique.

Dr. Brooks received his MD degree from Wayne State University in Detroit, and did his psychiatric residency at the University of Colorado in Denver. He is the co-author of the book *Ayurvedic Secrets to Longevity and Total Health* (Prentice Hall, 1996) and has authored many journal articles and book chapters on Ayurveda and mental health. He has published seminal research on the benefits of the Transcendental Meditation technique in the treatment of Vietnam veterans with post-traumatic stress. Dr. Brooks is an Adjunct Faculty member at Maharishi University of Management.

CPSIA information can be obtained
at www.ICGtesting.com
Printed in the USA
BVHW091924261120
593849BV00006B/12